Embedded Computer Systems for Space

Patrick H. Stakem

(c) October 2015

Number 7 in Space Series
3rd edition

ISBN - 9781520215914

Table of contents

Introduction

The book covers the topic of Embedded Computers for Spacecraft. We need to define and explore some terms, starting with "embedded computer." We'll look at its cpu, memory, and I/O. The Space environment is harsh, and hard on computer components. We'll review these effects, and see what additional requirements they place upon the system.

Just as embedded computers are special cases of computers in general, then space flight embedded computers are a special case of embedded. They are embedded computers which operate in a challenging environment.

I make the assumption you know a bit of computer architecture, how instructions are executed, and how cache works. If not, get a good book or two on computer architecture. There's some in the references. That's our starting point.

The flight software, both operating systems and application will be explored. In Space, software is the ideal component. It doesn't weigh anything, doesn't need gravity or air.

The environment the embedded system is operating in has a major impact on its design and implementation. The unit may be in Earth orbit, in orbit around another planet, on the surface of another planet, or traversing the solar system. Each of these environments is hostile to equipment, and each is different. Closer to the Sun means hotter, and more radiation. Farther away means less solar power. The large distances involved force slower bandwidth communication, and requires different protocols. In many cases, for long periods of time, spacecraft cannot communicate with Earth-based stations. Embedded computers are in just about anything we touch on a daily basis, our cars, our mobile phones and entertainment devices, most of our appliances, traffic light controllers – the list is nearly endless.

The earliest satellites did not have computers at all, but the technology quickly evolved to have special purpose-built units. Later, commercial microprocessors were employed, and many failed due to the radiation environment. Now, the latest technologies we use on Earth, multicore, graphics engines, non-volatile magnetic storage, FPGA's, are used in spacecraft electronics. The spacecraft have become networks of computers, or, nodes on a network of space assets.

This work has been compiled from sources that are ITAR compliant.

This 3rd edition has updates and corrections applied to the previous edition.

Author

The author received his BSEE from Carnegie Mellon University, and Masters in Computer Science and Applied Physics from the Johns Hopkins University. He has worked in the aerospace sector, supporting projects at all of the NASA Centers. He has taught for the graduate Engineering Science and Computer Science Departments at Loyola University in Maryland, and teaches Embedded Systems for the Johns Hopkins University, Whiting School of Engineering, Engineering for Professionals Program, and for Capitol Technology University. At Capitol, in the Summer of 2015, he co-taught Cubesat Engineering and Cubesat Operations courses.

Cover Photo by the author.

The StrongARM was developed by DEC for commercial use.. It flew on the Snap-1 mission, a British nanosat in low Earth Orbit, in the year 2000. It was part of a COTS spacecraft developed by Surrey Space Technology, Ltd.

What is Embedded?

First, we need to define an embedded system. Embedded computing refers to special purpose computers that are a part of a larger system, as opposed to generic desktop computers, tablets, and servers. Embedded systems are for specific purposes; they are not necessarily general purpose. They may have a limited or no human interface, but usually support complex I/O. They form the basis of all modern technical devices. Here, we are interested in the ones that are a part of a spacecraft.

The embedded computer can be characterized by the parameters of its central processing unit (CPU), memory, and input/output (I/O). The CPU parameters of importance are speed, power consumption, word size, and price. The memory parameters include power consumption, volatility, and size or capacity. I/O characteristics must be matched to those of external systems components.

I am assuming here that the reader is generally knowledgeable about how computers work, how instructions are executed, and Input-output is accomplished. There are many good books on these topics, some of which I included in the references.

The trend now is to include more than one CPU on the chip, called Multicore technology. In addition, specialized processor units for floating point, vector processing, and digital signal processing are included. Multicore changes the game.

Embedded systems have elements of hardware and software, and these are brought together into a working system. The systems engineering process, from requirements to testing and post-deployment support is discussed. There are known approaches that work. Software is a different animal than hardware, but the top-level principles for developing and testing derive from the same principles. Programmable hardware, in terms of FPGA's and SoC's introduce complexity, but can be addressed by the same engineering best practices.

Embedded systems have their own set of standards, and their own unique issues in security, but an embedded computer is also a computer. Virtualization and multicore technology have added new capabilities to embedded systems.

Many embedded systems are required to be real-time - they have strict deadlines. Others are event-driven - a trigger event kicks off a predetermined sequence of responses. Embedded systems are almost always resource constrained. The resources might be size, weight, power, throughput, heat generation, reliability, deadlines, etc. Embedded systems have a high non-recurring engineering (NRE) cost (development cost), but are generally cheap to produce in volume. Radiation tolerant units are much more expensive than their corresponding commercial grade units.

Embedded computer systems are constructed from monolithic microprocessor chips. Modern embedded systems might be Field Programmable Gate Array (FPGA)-based, or use a custom Application Specific Integrated Circuit (ASIC). Commodity pc boards can also form the basis of embedded system. It's just that embedded systems don't usually need or can take advantage of all the bells and whistles included with low-cost, mass-manufactured desktop computer boards.

Embedded systems can be found everywhere: refrigerators, the Space Shuttle, elevators, toothbrushes, vacuum cleaners, smartphones, automobiles, aircraft, running shoes, sewing machines, pacemakers, and more. There are a lot more embedded computers than general-purpose desktop, tablet, and server pc's. They are just sometimes harder to find.

The embedded computer can be characterized by the parameters of its central processing unit (CPU), memory, and input/output (I/O). The CPU parameters of importance are speed, power consumption, word size, and price. The memory parameters include power consumption, volatility, and size or capacity. I/O characteristics must be matched to external systems components.

Embedded processors

Very-low-cost, high-performance microprocessor-based embedded systems enable wide applications. Most of these boards, complete 32-bit computers with memory and I/O, cost less than $50. Add-on boards provide GPS location finding, wifi and bluetooth connectivity, 3-axis gyros, etc.

Advances driven by cellular phones and data systems have made available small powerful processors that rival a datacenter of a few years back. They are designed for communication, and include a variety of standard interfaces.

The devices are multicore, meaning there is more than one cpu. They can include specialty cores such as floating point or digital signal processing, They have memory integrated with the cpu. They support analog as well as digital interfaces. The boards tend of be deck-of-cards size or smaller, and typically cost under $50. Some examples include Arduino, Raspberry Pi, and BeagleBone boards.

Embedded microcontrollers have the cpu (or cpu's), memory, and I/O integrated onto one monolithic chip.

What are the concerns in Embedded Systems in any environment? – security, reliability, power, data communication. Radiation tolerant units are much more expensive than their corresponding commercial grade units.

Space environment

The space environment is hostile and non-forgiving. There is little or no gravity, so no convection cooling, leading to thermal problems. It is a high radiation environment. The system is power constrained. And, it is hard to debug and repair after launch.

There are differing environments by Mission type. For Near-Earth orbiters, there are the radiation problems of the Van Allen belts and South Atlantic Anomaly, and the issue of atmospheric drag. Missions were Shuttle serviceable, as long as the Shuttle fleet was available. Synchronous or L2 (Lagrange Point) missions are not fixable, at the present time. If we go towards the sun it gets hot. That includes missions to Venus or Mercury. If we go away from the sun, it gets cold, and the amount of energy we can capture via solar arrays is limited. This includes missions to the asteroids, Mars, Jupiter, Saturn, the outer planets, and their associated moons.

Planetary Probes include orbiters, rovers, and surface packages. There were Mercury and Venus landers (which tend to melt), Mars rovers and orbiters, Jovian and Saturnian moon probes, which have to deal with extreme radiation belts, and missions to the outer planets and beyond the solar system.

The functions of the embedded controllers on the spacecraft include navigation, attitude control and pointing, orbit control & maintenance, thermal control, energy management, and data management and communications (which may include antenna pointing).

Radiation Effects

There are two radiation problem areas: cumulative dose, and single event. Operating above the Van Allen belts of particles trapped in Earth's magnetic flux lines, spacecraft are exposed to the full fury of the Universe. Earth's magnetic poles do not align with the rotational poles, so the Van Allen belts dip to around 200 kilometers in the South Atlantic, leaving a region called the South Atlantic Anomaly. The magnetic field lines are good at deflecting charged particles, but mostly useless against electromagnetic radiation and uncharged particles such as neutrons. One trip across the Van Allen belts can ruin a spacecraft's electronics. Some spacecraft turn off sensitive electronics for several minutes every ninety minutes – every pass through the low dipping belts in the South Atlantic.

The Earth and other planets are constantly immersed in the solar wind, a flow of hot plasma emitted by the Sun in all directions, a result of the two-million-degree heat of the Sun's outermost layer, the Corona. The solar wind usually reaches Earth with a velocity around 400 km/s, with a density around 5 ions/cm^3. During magnetic storms on the Sun, flows can be several times faster, and stronger. The Sun tends to have an eleven year cycle of maxima. A solar flare is a large explosion in the Sun's atmosphere that can release as much as 6×10^{25} joules in one event, equal to about one sixth of the Sun's total energy output every second. Solar flares are frequently coincident with sun spots. Solar flares, being releases of large amounts of energy, can trigger Coronal Mass Ejections, and accelerate lighter particles to near the speed of light toward the planets.

The size of the Van Allen Belts shrink and expand in response to the Solar Wind. The wind is made up of particles, electrons up to 10 Million electron volts (MeV), and protons up to 100 Mev – all ionizing doses. One charged particle can knock thousands of electrons loose from the semiconductor lattice, causing noise, spikes, and current surges. Since memory elements are capacitors, they can be damaged or discharged, essentially changing state.

Vacuum tube based technology is essentially immune from radiation effects. The Russians designed (but did not complete) a Venus Rover mission using vacuum tube electronics. The Pioneer Venus spacecraft was launched into Venus orbit in 1978, and returned data until 1992. It did not use a computer, but an attitude controller built from discrete components.

Not that just current electronics are vulnerable. The Great Auroral Exhibition of 1859 interacted with the then-extant telegraph lines acting as antennae, such that batteries were not needed for the telegraph apparatus to operate for hours at a time. Some telegraph systems were set on fire, and operators shocked. The whole show is referred to as the Carrington Event, after amateur British Astronomer Richard Carrington.

Around other planets, the closer we get to the Sun, the bigger the impact of solar generated particles, and the less predictable they are. Auroras have been observed on Venus, in spite of the planet not having an observed magnetic field. The impact of the solar particles becomes less of a problem with the outer planets. Auroras have been observed on Mars, and the magnetic filed of Jupiter, Saturn, and some of the moons cause their "Van Allen belts" to trap large numbers of energetic particles, which cause more problems for spacecraft in transit. Both Jupiter and Saturn have magnetic field greater than Earth's. Not all planets have a magnetic field, so not all have charged particle belts.

Radiation Hardness Issues for Space Flight Applications

A complete discussion of the physics of radiation damage to semiconductors is beyond the scope of this document. However, an overview of the subject is presented. The tolerance of semiconductor devices to radiation must be examined in the light of their damage susceptibility. The problems fall into two broad categories, those caused by cumulative dose, and those transient events caused by asynchronous very energetic particles, such as those experienced during a period of intense solar flare activity. The unit of absorbed dose of radiation is the *rad*, representing the absorption of 100 ergs of energy per gram of material. A kilo-rad is one thousand rads. At 10k rad, death in humans is almost instantaneous. One hundred kilo-rad is typical in the vicinity of Jupiter's radiation belts. Ten to twenty kilo-rad is typical for spacecraft in low Earth orbit, but the number depends on how much time the spacecraft spends outside the Van Allen belts, which act as a shield by trapping energetic particles.

Absorbed radiation can cause temporary or permanent changes in the semiconductor material. Usually neutrons, being uncharged, do minimal damage, but energetic protons and electrons cause lattice or ionization damage in the material, and resultant parametric changes. For example, the leakage current can increase, or bit states can change. Certain technologies

11

and manufacturing processes are known to produce devices that are less susceptible to damage than others. More expensive substrate materials such as diamond or sapphire help to make the device more tolerant of radiation, but much more expensive.

Radiation tolerance of 100 kilo-rad is usually more than adequate for low Earth orbit (LEO) missions that spend most of their life below the shielding of the Van Allen belts. For Polar missions, a higher total dose is expected, from 100k to 1 mega-rad per year. For synchronous, equatorial orbits, that are used by many communication satellites, and some weather satellites, the expected dose is several kilo-rad per year. Finally, for planetary missions to Venus, Mars, Jupiter, Saturn, and beyond, requirements that are even more stringent must be met. For one thing, the missions usually are unique, and the cost of failure is high. For missions towards the sun, the higher fluence of solar radiation must be taken into account. The larger outer planets, such as Jupiter and Saturn, have their own large radiation belts around them as well.

Cumulative radiation dose causes a charge trapping in the oxide layers, which manifests as a parametric change in the devices. Total dose effects may be a function of the dose rate, and annealing of the device may occur, especially at elevated temperatures. Annealing refers to the self-healing of radiation induced defects. This can take minutes to months, and is not applicable for lattice damage. The internal memory or registers of the cpu are the most susceptible area of the chip, and are usually deactivated for operations in a radiation environment. The gross indication of radiation damage is the increased power consumption of the device, and one researcher reported a doubling of the power consumption at failure. In addition, failed devices would operate at a lower clock rate, leading to speculation that a key timing parameter was being effected in this case.

Single event upsets (seu's) are the response of the device to direct high energy isotropic flux, such as cosmic rays, or the secondary effects of high energy particles colliding with other matter (such as shielding). Large transient currents may result, causing changes in logic state (bit flips), unforeseen operation, device latch-up, or burnout. The transient currents can be monitored as an indicator of the onset of SEU problems. After SEU, the results on the operation of the processor are unpredictable. Mitigation of problems caused by SEU's involves self-test, memory scrubbing, and forced resets.

The LET (linear energy transfer) is a measure of the incoming particles' delivery of ionizing energy to the device. Latch-up refers to the inadvertent operation of a parasitic SCR (silicon control rectifier), triggered by ionizing radiation. In the area of latch-up, the chip can be made inherently hard due to use of the Epitaxial process for fabrication of the base layer. Even the use of an Epitaxial layer does not guarantee complete freedom from latch-up, however. The next step generally involves a silicon on insulator (SOI) or Silicon on Sapphire (SOS) approach, where the substrate is totally insulated, and latch-ups are not possible. This is an expensive approach,

In some cases, shielding is effective, because even a few millimeters of aluminum can stop electrons and protons. However, with highly energetic or massive particles (such as alpha particles, helium nuclei), shielding can be counter-productive. When the atoms in the shielding are hit by an energetic particle, a cascade of lower energy, lower mass particles results. These can cause as much or more damage than the original source particle.

Cumulative dose and single events

The more radiation that the equipment gets, in low does for a long time, or in high does for a shorter time, the greater the probability of damage.

These events are caused by high energy particles, usually protons, that disrupt and damage the semiconductor lattice. The effects can be upsets (bit changes) or latch-ups (bit stuck). The damage can "heal" itself, but its often permanent. Most of the problems are caused by energetic solar protons, although galactic cosmic rays are also an issue. Solar activity varies, but is now monitored by sentinel spacecraft, and periods of intensive solar radiation and particle flux can be predicted. Although the Sun is only 8 light minutes away from Earth, the energetic particles travel much slower than light, and we have several days warning. During periods of intense solar activity, Coronal Mass Ejection (CME) events can send massive streams of charged particles outward. These hit the Earth's magnetic field and create a bow wave. The Aurora Borealis or Northern Lights are one manifestation of incoming charged particles hitting the upper reaches of the ionosphere.

Cosmic rays, particles and electromagnetic radiation, are omni-directional, and come from extra-solar sources. Most of them, 85%, are protons, with gamma rays and x-rays thrown in the mix. Energy levels range to 10^6 to 10^8 electron volts (eV). These are mostly filtered out by Earth's atmosphere.

There is no such mechanism on the Moon, where they reach and interact with the surface material. Solar flux energy's range to several Billion electron volts (Gev).

Other interesting problems plague advanced electronics off-planet. The Hughes (Boeing) HS 601 series of communications spacecraft suffered a series of failures in 1992-1995 due to relays. In zero gravity, tin "whiskers" grew within the units, causing them to short. The control processors on six spacecraft were effected, with three mission failures because both computers failed. This was highly noticeable, as the satellites were communication relays for television. The Whisker phenomenon is now well understood.

The effects of radiation on silicon circuits can be mitigated by redundancy, the use of specifically radiation hardened parts, Error Detection and Correction (EDAC) circuitry, and scrubbing techniques. Hardened chips are produced on special insulating substrates such as Sapphire. Bipolar technology chips can withstand radiation better than CMOS technology chips, at the cost of greatly increased power consumption. Shielding techniques are also applied.

EDAC can be done with hardware or software, but always carries a cost in time and complexity. A longer word than needed for the data item allows for the inclusion of error detecting and correcting codes. The simplest scheme is a parity bit, which can detect single bit (or an odd number of errors, but can't correct anything. EDAC is applied to memory and I/O, particularly the uplink and downlink.

Mitigation Techniques

The effects of radiation on silicon circuits can be mitigated by redundancy, the use of specifically radiation hardened parts, Error Detection and Correction (EDAC) circuitry, and scrubbing techniques. Hardened chips are produced on special insulating substrates such as Sapphire. Bipolar technology chips can withstand radiation better than CMOS technology chips, at the cost of greatly increased power consumption. Shielding techniques are also applied. In error detection and correction techniques, special encoding of the stored information provides a protection against flipped bits, at the cost of additional bits to store. Redundancy can also be applied at the device or box level, with the popular Triple Modular Redundancy (TMR) technique triplicating everything, and based on the assumption that the probability of a double failure is less than that of a single failure. Watchdog timers are used to reset systems unless they are themselves reset by the software. Of course, the watchdog timer circuitry is also susceptible to failure.

Thermal issues

Radiation is not the only problem. In space, things are either too hot or too cold. On the inner planets toward the Sun, things are too hot. On the planets outward of Earth, things are too cold. In space, there is no gravity, so there are no convection currents. Cooling is by conduction and radiation only. This requires heat-generating electronics to have a conductive path to a radiator. That makes board design for chips, and chip packaging, complex and expensive.

Parts can be damaged by excessive heat, both ambient and self-generated. In a condition known as *thermal runaway*, an uncontrolled positive feedback situation is created, where overheating causes the part to further overheat, and fail faster.

Mechanical issues

In zero gravity, every thing floats, whether you want it to or not. Floating conductive particles, bits of solder or bonding wire, can short out circuitry. This is mitigated by conformal coatings, but the perimeter of the die is usually maintained at ground potential, and cannot be coated due to the manufacturing sequence.

The challenges of electronics in space are daunting, but much is now understood about the failure mechanisms, and techniques to address them.

ESD sensitivity

Solid state devices are particularly susceptible to *electrostatic discharge* (ESD) effects. These effects can involve very large voltages that cause device breakdown. Certain semiconductor lattice structures that have been damaged can actually "heal" over time, a process called annealing. Passive parts are sensitive to ESD as well. As parts are made smaller, the susceptibility to ESD effects increases. Proper grounding helps with ESD, providing a consistent voltage across components, without significant differences.

ESD can cause parametric changes, which shift the device out of its nominal tolerance region. Over time, parametric changes may go unnoticed as they build, and lead to sudden catastrophic failure.

Bad Parts

Another issue is substandard parts, manufactured with an eye to low price and increased sales. Some of these are reversed-engineered or pirated parts. They may bear the same markings and internal identification codes as the legitimate part, and are difficult to tell from the genuine article. This becomes a major problem in military and aerospace applications, although commercial systems are also vulnerable. Software is also subject to "knock-off" versions.

Besides a reliability issue, counterfeit parts cause security concerns in critical systems. A major player in the identification of counterfeit parts is the University of Maryland's Center for Advanced Life Cycle Engineering. It has found that a major source of problems is the large volume of "scrap" electronics sent overseas for recycling and disposal.

Programs such as the Trusted Integrated Circuit (TIC), aim to develop new approaches to test and ensure the integrity of such components.

A counterfeit highly complex chip is hard to detect. You could examine the chip die for full compliance with the design specification, but this is expensive. You could check the product ID on the chip, but this can certainly be faked.

A cheap knock-off chip can be marked properly, and pass functional tests, but fail early due to production issues. Malicious circuitry/code can be included, locked away and hidden from view. Depending on the requirements of the embedded device, get the paper trail and buy from a trusted supplier. Be aware of the problem.

Tin Whiskers

In 1998, the on-orbit Galaxy IV satellite's main control computer failed due to tin whiskers. This is a phenomena where, with the use of predominately tin solder, small conductive tendrils grow due to compressive stress, and cause electrical shorts. This occurs in several other metals as well. This phenomena was noted early in the vacuum tube era. It can be mitigated by adding lead to the solder, a practice that is now banned. Tin whisker problems have been noted in heart pacemakers, and a false alarm at the Millstone Nuclear Plant in 2005

Flight Hardware

The spacecraft computer(s) will have a variety of jobs to do. Before we examine the hardware in detail, let's look at what has to be done.

The spacecraft is operating in a hostile environment, and is on it's own in terms of power and communication. It will have to keep its solar arrays pointed at the Sun to keep the batteries charged. It needs to keep its communication antennas pointed at Earth, or to a relay satellite. It will have to monitor and adjust it's temperature as its orientation to the Sun changes throughout the orbit. And, it will have to complete the mission it was designed to do – observing the Earth or other planets or the sun, or serving as a communication relay.

Generally, the spacecraft is thought of as having two parts, the bus, and the payload. The bus is the platform with all the engineering systems on it. The payload is one or more science instruments, or perhaps a communications section for streaming television. The bus portion can be generic, with different payloads for different missions. This saves money, and simplifies production. It enhances safety and mission lifetime, by using proven approaches and hardware. The bus section provides services to the payload, such as pointing, thermal control, electrical power, and command and telemetry.

The payload will have its own computers. If we have a communications relay spacecraft, the receiver units will likely use software-defined radio, which is a computer application. If we have a science instruments, it needs to be pointed properly, configured, and monitored. If there is onboard data processing, it would be done in a dedicated instrument computer.

We will limit our coverage mostly to the flight computer on the spacecraft bus. The instrument computer will have its own unique set of requirements, and will differ among instrument sets. It focuses on servicing the instrument, and collecting the data. The bus computer has a range of engineering tasks to run, almost the same across many spacecraft types.

CPUs

Soon after their development, general purpose microprocessors were used in embedded roles. Eventually, most chip manufacturers produced special models of embedded chips, allowing the use of their standard software tools, but including lower power modes with special capabilities for the embedded world. Many of these found application on spacecraft. The harsh environment of space imposed particular requirements on the chips, in the areas of vibration and shock tolerance for the launch phase, and temperature and radiation tolerance during the operational lifetime. The use of embedded computers on space evolved from purpose-built units to the early 4- and 8- bit processors, through 16-bit to 32 bit processors, and to special rad-hard versions of these.

The 4-bit Intel 4004 was used on the Pioneer-10 Deep Space Mission, launched in 1972. The mission studied the asteroid belt, the solar wind, Jupiter, and the outer reaches of the solar system. The computer was used to hold, decode, and distribute commands transmitted from Earth. The mission lasted until 2003, when communications was lost due to distance, a mission duration of 30 years. As of March 2011, the spacecraft was some 102 Astronomical Units (AU= 93 million miles) from the Sun, where sunlight takes 14 hours traverse the distance. The last successful reception of telemetry was on April 27, 2002; subsequent signals provided no usable data. The final signal from *Pioneer 10* was received on January 23, 2003 when it was 12 billion kilometers (80 AU) from Earth.

Advanced architectures

This section discusses computation units for other than integers. These can be implemented with co-processors, but are increasingly found on the same semiconductor die as the main integer processor.

Floating Point

Floating point involves the calculation of engineering and scientific data beyond what integer processing units can support. Floating point is a lot like engineering/scientific calculation, where we have a fixed size mantissa, and an exponent. Without going into a lot of messy math, let's look at a simple view of this process.

A *byte* is a collection of 8 bits. This makes for a handy size. In binary, a byte can represent 1 of 256 (2^8) possible states or values. Computer arithmetic is a binary positional notation. What we use ourselves is a decimal positional notation. Any number can be sued for the base. Computer like 2, we like 10.

A computer *word* is a collection of 8, 16, 24, 32, or some other number of bits. The number of bits collected into a word does not need to be a power of two. The range of numbers we can represent depends on how many bits we have in the word. Integers have a lsb weight of 1, and a range of $2^{\text{number of bits}}$. If we want signed quantities, we must give up one of our position bits to hold the sign. We can get fancy, and use a scaled integer, with the binary point in the middle of the word, but we have created a bookkeeping problem for ourselves.

The standard integer add, subtract, multiply, and divide operations implemented in the ALU (arithmetic logic unit) assume the binary point is on the right side of the word. The IEEE-754 standard for floating point is the accepted definition of numbers, operations on numbers, and the handling of underflow and overflow.

In a finite word length machine, there is a tradeoff between dynamic range and accuracy in representation. The value of the most significant bit sets the dynamic range because the effective value of the most positive number is infinity. The value of the least significant bit sets the accuracy, because a value less than the LSB is zero. And, the MSB and the LSB are related by the word length. We can implement our own extended integer scheme, using 3 bytes (24 bit), or 8 bytes (64 bits), or whatever we choose. It is then up to us to implement the math functions, because the ones built into the cpu won't work for us anymore.

On 8-bit processors, it is possible to use a floating point library, but this will be very slow in operation. Most 32-bit processors these days have an integral hardware floating point unit.

The standard QNX Neutrino libraries are compiled to use a soft-float implementation for floating-point operations to ensure the code can run on all supported ARM processors. The soft-float implementation passes floating-point arguments and results in ARM registers, or on the stack.

Graphics Processing Unit (GPU)

A GPU is a specialized computer architecture to manipulate image data at high rates. It can be a single chip, or incorporated with a general purpose CPU. The GPU devices are highly parallel, and specifically designed to handle image data, and operations on that data. They do this much fastest than a programmed general purpose CPU. Most desktop machines have the GPU function on a video card or integrated with their CPU. Originally, GPU's were circuit card based. GPU operations are very memory intensive. The GPU design is customized to (Single Instruction, Multiple Data) SIMD type operations.

The instruction set of the GPU is specific to graphics operations on block data. The requirements were driven by the demands of 2-D and 3-D video games on pc's, phones, tablets, and dedicated gaming units. As GPU units became faster and more capable, they began to consume more power (and thus generate more heat) than the associated CPU's. They are applicable to many classes of Science Data processing.

Although designed to process video data, some GPU's have been used as adjunct data processors and accelerators in other areas involving vectors and matrices, such as the inverse discrete cosine transform. Types of higher-level processing implemented by GPU's include texture mapping, polygon rendering, object rotation, and coordination system transformation. They also support object shading operations, data oversampling, and interpolation. GPU's find a major application area in video decoding. Building on this, GPU's enable advanced features in digital cameras. These features are supported by Image Processing Libraries. This can be employed in star-tracking cameras, and to facilitate orbit and attitude calculations.

Vector Processor

Vector processing involves the processing of vectors of related data, in a (single instruction, multiple data) *SIMD*_mode. For example, vector addition is an SIMD operation.

SIMD refers to a class of parallel computers that perform the same operations on multiple data items simultaneously. This is data level parallelism, which is found in multimedia (video and audio) data used in gaming applications. The

SIMD approach evolved from the vector supercomputers of the 1970's, which operated upon a vector of data with a single operation. Sun Microsystems introduced SIMD operations in their SPARC architecture in 1995. A popular application of SIMD architecture is Intel's MMX (Multimedia Extensions) instruction set circa 1996 for the X-86 architecture.

Digital Signal Processor

Digital signal processors resemble computers in many ways, and come in embedded versions. They handle specialized data types, and include special-purpose operations derived from the digital signal processing realm. This includes the Multiply-and-Add (mac), a digital filtering primitive. Digital signal processing finds application with the processing of audio and video data.

A Digital Signal Processor (DSP) is similar to a general purpose CPU, but provides specialized operations for DSP-type operations on specialized data formats. Originally, the DSP function was implemented by software running in a CPU. DSP operations usually have time deadline constraints (hard real time requirements).

Mobile phones and cable modems, to name two examples, drove the development of faster, dedicated hardware units. The first practical commercial product based on a DSP chip was Texas Instrument's Speak-n-Spell toy. Before that, the military applications of sonar and radar data processing drove the technology.

The nature of digital domain signal data and filtering require some unique architectural features. Hardware modulo addressing and bit-reversed addressing is used in digital filtering. Operations on data tend to be SIMD. The *Multiply-Accumulate* primitive is the basis for digital filter implementation. Saturation arithmetic is used to prevent overflow. Both fixed point and floating point data are used. A three-memory Harvard architecture allows simultaneous access of an opcode and two operands.
Multicore chips for DSP are now common. These fast DSP's have enabled new technologies and applications such as software-defined radio.

An illustrative device is Analog Devices' Blackfin series of embedded DSP's. These chips are supported by a real-time operating systems. The Blackfin is a

32-bit RISC processor with dual 16-bit multiply/accumulate (MAC) units, and provision for 8-bit video processing in real-time.

Some ARM chips such as the Cortex-8 family, and the OMAP3 processors include both a general purpose CPU, and a DSP.

The Zynq FPGA has an integral ARM processor, and can form the basis of a Software defined radio unit.

Viterbi Processor

A *Viterbi decoder* is used on a bit stream that has been encoded using a convolutional code for error correction to achieve reliable data transfer. The technique was developed by Andrew Viterbi in the late 1960's. Convolution codes operate close to the theoretical Shannon limit, although better codes have since been developed. The Shannon limit is the maximum rate of information transfer possible in a given noisy channel. Viterbi encoding is quite common in spacecraft command and telemetry streams.

Originally implemented in software on a general purpose CPU, and later on DSP's, Viterbi-specific hardware chips are now available. The technique is used for error control in transmitted data.

An example hardware instantiation is the Texas Instruments TMS320C6418 DSP chip, with Viterbi co-processor. The chip has 0.5 megabyte of level 2 cache included with a DSP CPU, and the Viterbi unit. The DSP can achieve rates of 2.4 billion multiply-accumulate operations per second. The chip includes two serial ports, two audio ports, dual I^2C control ports, and the memory interface.

Multicore

We can compare multicore devices to the large parallel machines of some 10 years past, in the same sense that we can compare a single-chip cpu to large mainframe systems of 20-25 years ago. The architecture is similar, but the implementation is different due to changing technologies.

Multicore techniques are now being applied to embedded processors as well.

This enables some techniques that were not previously available. In the embedded world, the cores do not necessarily need to be the same. Actually, this technique was used when to Intel floating point co-processor, the 80387, was incorporated onto the same chip as the integer processor, the 80386, in the design of the follow-on 80486 chip. Today, multiple integer cores can share the same silicon substrate with specialized floating point, digital signal and vector processing, and specialized media and video engines. The individual cores can implement superscalar, super-pipelined, or other optimization techniques. We have a MIMD (multiple instruction, multiple data) parallel processing chip for embedded applications. Nothing is ever free, though. The challenge is in the programming.

The latest ARM architecture for embedded supports multicore (currently, up to 8-core) 64-bit devices. Both symmetrical and asymmetrical implementations are included. Putting a lot of cores on a single substrate is challenging, and getting them to work together co-operatively and non-intrusively is difficult. The CoreLink cache coherent interconnect system, for use in multicore applications, is one emerging solution. Some problems are inherently parallelizable, but most are not. Not many problem domains scale linearly with the amount of computing horsepower available. Such *embarrassingly parallel* applications are rarely of practical interest.

Spacecraft-on-a-chip

In the limit, the spacecraft can be implemented on a single chip. A feasibility study was done by the University of Surrey (U.K.) for the U. S. Air Force in 2006. The computer is the vehicle. Your cellphone probably has a 3-axis accelerometer, a magnetometer, a GPS unit, a gyroscope, a camera, and a high end embedded processor. A phonesat went into orbit in 2013, using a Google Nexus One. It was integrated with a 3-unit (3U) Cubesat called STRaND-1 from Surrey Space Technology.

But we can get smaller than that. As the electronics gets implemented on denser and denser structures, we can get the processor, memory, input-output, and MEMS sensors on one piece of silicon. They can also economically be be produced in quantity, and deployed in swarms. They would be disposable. This concept is under development at numerous locations.

These small spacecraft would be deployed on orbit for targets of opportunity, such as a solar flare. We can envision a swarm of such chipsats, interacting by short range radio, and clustering as necessary.

Embedded Peripherals

Early in the implementation of microprocessors, it was hard to fit even the 8-bit cpu on a single piece of silicon. As the technology became more advanced, it was common to incorporate more and more functionality onto the same chip. Functions such as interrupt control, dma control, dynamic memory refresh, and floating point operations, that had originally required separate chips, were now merged with the cpu. This reduced the system chip count, speeded up operations, and reduced cost. This was an ideal situation for embedded processors, as it enabled single-chip solutions in many cases. This section discusses the peripheral functionality brought onto the same chip as the cpu. In addition, both ROM and RAM (and now, flash) are incorporated on the same device, in varying combinations.

Counter/Timer

This multipurpose peripheral is invaluable in embedded systems. In timer mode, the input clock is the system or cpu clock. The counter is preloaded with a value, and counts down. When the count reaches zero, an interrupt is generated, and the counter register is reloaded. For example, with an 8-bit counter, if it is pre-loaded with 128, it generates a square wave at a system clock/256 rate. This allows periodic interrupts at sub-multiples of the system clock, and synchronous with it. We can also increment a second counter upon each interrupt to handle longer periods of elapsed time.

In counter mode, the clock comes from an external source, and is asynchronous to the system clock. For example, we might use the output stream of pulses from an optical encoder. Another application might be as the Baud rate clock for a serial I/O line.

Since the counter/timer usually has multiple channels, we might use one channel to generate a known time base, and other units for counting.

Examples of legacy stand-alone counter/timer chips are the Intel 8253 and 8254. These were used along with the 8088/8086 cpu's in the IBM pc architecture in 1981. The functionality is now incorporated in motherboard hardware ("southbridge"). These chips have three 16-bit independent counters. Their outputs are usually connected to system interrupts. In the pc architecture, counter 1 is used for real-time keeping, timer 2 handles dram refresh, and timer 3 generates tones on the system speaker. The counters are handled like standard peripherals for sending command words, and reading status. They are generally mapped into the I/O space.

Several modes of operation are supported. In mode 0, the counter generates an interrupt at the terminal count. In mode 1, the timer functions as a programmable one-shot generator. In mode 2, the device is a divide-by-n counter, to generate real-time clock ticks. In mode 3, it functions as a square wave generator. In mode 4 the output remains in a high state until the count is reached, drops low for one clock cycle, then returns to the high state. In mode 5, the count is initiated by an external control signal.

A special-purpose timer essential for embedded applications is the Watchdog. This is a free-running timer that generates a cpu reset unless it is reset by the software. This helps to ensure that the system doesn't lock up during certain critical time periods, and the software is meeting its deadlines. This approach has saved many a system.

The watchdog timer is implemented in hardware, and does it's jobs without direct software intervention. If the software fails to reset the timer, the system reboots. This might simply reset operations and restart, or may include diagnostics before the system is restarted.

If the watchdog is not reset, it generates an interrupt to reset the host. This should take the system back to a baseline state, and restart it. Hopefully, normal operations will resume. The embedded system can't rely on a human operator to notice a fault in the operations or a "hung" system, and press the reset button. Many *very remote* systems, such as those in deep water or on the surface of other planets have successfully recovered from faults with a watchdog.

Time permitting, it is useful to checkpoint the state of the system before the reset is made, to assist in diagnostics.

In some architectures, a second system runs in parallel with the primary, and results are compared. If the second system detects a difference, both systems are reset. What happens when the diagnostic hardware/software makes a mistake? This has happened, where the backup system thinks the primary system has made a mistake, and takes over, erroneously. This has resulted in the loss of launch vehicles.

A preferred approach, which is hardware-intensive, is to use three identical systems, with voting logic. The majority wins. The approach is based on the fact that double errors are less likely than single errors. But, who watches the watchdogs, the watchcat?

Sometimes the system cannot be shut down, even in the case of an error. A simple hardwired fail-safe backup system may be activated, or other corrective actions can be taken. In the case where the system has to operate through a failure, the term melt-before-fail is sometimes used.

JTAG support

Joint Test Action Group (JTAG) is the name for the IEEE-1149.1 standard for a test access point and a boundary scan architecture for integrated circuit level debug. The JTAG effort began in 1985 as a test and fault isolation methodology for board level products. It is particularly valuable for embedded systems, with limited human interfaces for visibility. It is used in cpu-based systems, FPGA's, and SoC architectures. With the proper application software, the JTAG can access and control test instrumentation included within the chip. JTAG can also be used to load data into internal flash memory. JTAG is used a portal to the chips built-in self test (BIST).

JTAG uses a 4-wire interface (data in, data out, clock, mode select), sometimes with a 5th line, test reset. The data transfer mode is serial, using a short cable. The host side for the JTAG system can be connected via USB or even Ethernet. There are numerous commercial JTAG tool vendors providing multi-platform support, and Open Source tools also exist. Almost all modern embedded architectures provide JTAG support. A 2-wire alternative is Serial Wire Debug, that has the JTAG protocol implemented,

Harness

Harness refers to the wiring interconnect, the power and data backbone between connections. The harness will also include connectors. In the harness, the wires must be the right rating ("gage") and, like anything else, derated. There is usually a series of "break-out boxes" for each connector, to allow access to signals and power, but also to minimize the number of physical connector mate/demate cycles. There is a "safe-to-mate" procedure that, among other things, will have you verify that power is off before connection. It is a good practice to log the number of connects and disconnects of connector pairs.

SoC and FPGA

Field Programmable Gate Arrays are integrated circuits that are programmable or configurable at the hardware level. The devices are ideal for high density embedded designs. This configuration defines the interconnect between standard logic blocks on the device. The logic blocks can also be configurable. The device can be set up to be programmed once, or capable of being programmed multiple times. In the limit, the device can be reconfigured on the fly, as it is operating. An FPGA gives us configurable instead of fixed hardware. A traditional CPU provides fixed hardware from the manufacturer that we can direct with a software program in terms of operations on data, and the sequence of these operations. It supports data-dependent branches. With an FPGA, we have "programmable" or configurable hardware as well. Each reconfiguration results in a new and different architecture.

An *ASIC*, or Application Specific Integrated Circuit, gives us the ability to design and have fabricated a complex logic circuit. The design tools and simulator can be hosted on desktop tools, and we send the design tool to a semiconductor fabrication service. In return, we get packaged chips. The design better be right, as the cost of a design change in terms of dollars and time is high. The *non-recurring engineering* (NRE) can range into the hundreds of thousands of dollars. The advantage of the ASIC is that we get a custom hardware design for our particular problem. It is possible to include analog parts as well as digital. The ASIC will be purpose-built for the particular application. Complexity levels of 100 million gates have been achieved. Mixed-signal ASIC's permit both analog and digital devices on the same substrate. Standard design tools allow for output of design files to fabrication services such as *MOSIS* (Metal Oxide Semiconductor Implementation Service).

The ASIC is designed specifically for the application, and is "lean and mean," not containing anything else. The functionality is captured in a Hardware Description Language. An AISC can implement a CPU as part of its structure. With complexity at this level, the ASIC may be referred to a

System-on-Chip (SoC) architecture. It can contain hundreds of millions of logic gates.

In mechanical terms, the ASIC represents a system cut from a single piece of metal. The FPGA would represent the same system constructed from standardized components and fasteners.

FPGA's consist of millions of logic gates. They are easily modified, and design changes have a small NRE cost. One can implement a CPU on an FPGA. This may not be the most efficient architectural approach. Most of the designs involve the use of standard library components, or purchased or open source *IPC* – Intellectual Property Cores.

IP Cores are design files allowing for instantiation of standard components in an ASIC or FPGA. A large market has developed in the marketing and licensing of IP Cores. The advantage of the IP Core from a reputable source is the standardized design file that has been verified. Cores for I/O functions and complete processors are available. Cores can contain both analog and digital functions. Open source IP cores are available. These allow for modification of the design. The ARM processor, among others, is available as an IP core.

With an FPGA, we can match the architecture to the problem in a better way than applying a commodity CPU. For example, the input data format might require 13 bits. We can do this job with a 16-bit machine, or we can build a 13-bit ALU in the FPGA.

An *ASIC*, or Application Specific Integrated Circuit, gives us the ability to design and have fabricated a complex logic circuit. The design tools and simulator can be hosted on desktop tools, and we send the design tool to a semiconductor fabrication service. In return, we get packaged chips. The design better be right, as the cost of a design change in terms of dollars and time is high. The *non-recurring engineering* (NRE) can range into the hundreds of thousands of dollars. The advantage of the ASIC is that we get a custom hardware design for our particular problem. It is possible to include analog parts as well as digital. The ASIC will be purpose-built for the particular application. Complexity levels of 100 million gates have been achieved. Mixed-signal ASIC's permit both analog and digital devices on the same substrate. Standard design tools allow for output of design files to fabrication services such as *MOSIS* (Metal Oxide Semiconductor Implementation Service).

The ASIC is designed specifically for the application, and is "lean and mean," not containing anything else. The functionality is captured in a Hardware Description Language. An AISC can implement a CPU as part of its structure. With complexity at this level, the ASIC may be referred to a *System-on-Chip* (SoC) architecture. It can contain hundreds of millions of logic gates.

In mechanical terms, the ASIC represents a system cut from a single piece of metal. The FPGA would represent the same system constructed from standardized components and fasteners.

ASIC's have been around since the 1980's. Large libraries of functions have been developed that are purchasable or available in open source. Standard cells are used in the implementation, ensuring known and well-characterized devices.

Generally, FPGA's are slower and less energy efficient than ASIC's, but that is changing as FPGA technology matures.

For an FPGA or ASIC, with an embedded CPU core, the final device will be a chip on a board, so both the chip design and the board design need to be captured. The chip design pinout will influence the board design.

If the ASIC or FPGA includes a CPU core, there will be associated software. This development process is identical to that of any software programmable device, and is illustrated on the top of the diagram. We produce code in a higher-level language such as c, using library routines for common functions. Some assembly language may be included in-line or as separate modules. These are linked together into one software load of binary executable code.

We need a new word for the configuration information for the FPGA or ASIC. The preferred word is *configware*. It is not hardware, software, or firmware. The configware captures the device configuration. It is possible to translate c code to configware, essentially, compiling a program into hardware. This process is not always successful, and fails to exploit the inherent parallelism of the hardware, because of the lack of parallelism in the language. The hardware can also be specified directly in a hardware description language such as *VHDL* (Very High Level Design language). From this description, a synthesizer software tool produces a place-and-route description of the chip. FPGAs particularly use standardized logic blocks or modules, at a level of complexity above the gate level. The configuration of these modules, and their interconnect, is captured, as well as the I/O connection to the device's pins. This results in a binary file, akin to the binary machine language file from the software assembly process. At this point, we have a definition of the synthesized hardware.

From the pinout of the device, we can design a printed circuit board (pcb) to hold the chips, using industry standard board layout tools. We also do a power and signal integrity analysis at this level. This gives us an implementable design that is electrically and physically correct. From the pcb layout files, we can get a board manufactured.

VHDL code can be used to design the hardware of the chip for instantiation into a manufactured ASIC. This has a high NRE cost. We can also define a One-Time Configurable (OTC) FPGA target. Most interestingly, we can target a reconfigurable FPGA, which we can program at our own development facility. What is important to realize is that the device can also be reconfigured dynamically. If the ASIC is like ROM, then the FPGA is like flash. The software-based tools that produce software code from higher-level abstractions are called compilers. The software-based tools that produce hardware configuration files from higher-level abstractions are called synthesizers.

The reconfiguration property is critical – reconfigurable FPGA's give us the ability to change the basic computing structure even on the fly. This opens new capabilities, but brings along with it a level of complexity that must be considered. If self-modifying code is a difficult concept, self-modifying hardware is even more so.

A system-on-chip (SoC) approach includes the processor, memory, and I/O on a single substrate. These may also be on different die in the same package. Analog and radio frequency parts can be included. The SoC is a "one-chip" solution. As semiconductor manufacturing technology advances, more functionality can be provided on a single chip. An alternative approach is the System in a Package (SiP), which integrates multiple chips in one package.

Most SOC design starts with IP cores and hardware blocks that are prequalified and tested. These can be combined in the design with memory cores, and specific I/O cores such as USB and CAN. Each core IP comes with its own license terms and restrictions. SOC's can be fabricated as full custom chips, in standard cells, and in FPGA's. The non-recurring engineering costs are higher for the SOC approach, but it can result in a highly optimized design in terms of space, power, and reliability. Standard cell libraries are readily available. These have the advantage of having been tested in silicon, and target specific silicon foundry's and processes.

IP Cores

An *intellectual property (IP)* core is a reusable logic unit that can be licensed, owned, and included in a design. IP cores can be used as building blocks for ASIC's, FPGA's, and Soc's. The discussion in the software section regarding proprietary versus open source applies. IP cores can also be proprietary or open source. Cores as a product are available in hardware description language form, essentially, source code for hardware. Proprietary cores may or may not be modifiable, and may or may not be supported by the vendor. Cores may also be available as netlist files, which are a Boolean algebra representation that has to be instantiated in a specific technology. A gate level netlist is seen as analogous to assembly language, and is portable to any process (implementation) technology.

The cores can contain digital and analog components, but the analog components require specific transistor layout formats. Complete embedded processors such as the 8-bit Intel 8051 series and various members of the ARM family are available as cores. Besides entire cpu's, IP cores are available for various interfaces and I/O devices. Individual developers can produce cores, and include them in libraries.

The intellectual property owner, the developer of the core, sees a return on his NRE cost of developing the hardware, and can have the design used in a large number of application areas, perhaps leading to an industry standard or industry-preferred approach. Core vendors are wary of reverse engineering of their core, just as software suppliers are concerned with the same process in their domain. Open Source cores are available.

Hard cores are defined at a physical layer, and provide a predictable performance. They are supplied as transistor-level layout format. This is subject to using a particular target chip foundry. Generally, a hard core cannot be changed. It represents a plug-in function. Soft cores, on the other hand, are specified in the RTL language, or as a netlist, and are "compiled" into a design. They can be easily changed by industry-standard toolsets. The design is portable, with respect to a fabrication technology.

CPU cores are readily available for popular CPU architectures. A PCIexpress bus core is available, as well as Ethernet, CAN bus, usb, and other standards. Various cores to address specific application areas such as DSP are also available.

Memory

Embedded systems, although usually resource constrained, can make use of commodity static and dynamic random access memory (ram). For space systems, we need special technology to provide redundancy. Memory is susceptible to radiation anomalies.

Solid state mass memories devices can be incorporated into embedded systems. Spacecraft systems do not employ rotating magnetic memory, because of the resulting momentum bias. Flash memory is the medium of choice.

MRAM is an interesting emerging technology for radiation environments. The storage mechanism is more tolerant to radiation, although the surrounding circuitry is not. MRAM is magnetorestrictive random access memory, essentially, vintage core memory in integrated circuit form. It can be used in place of semiconductor flash memory, and can have a serial or parallel interface. Unlike flash, it has unlimited write capability, and can write individual bits.

There are many types of memory used with current cpu's. Most memory types are supported, if the word sizes and timing match. There is a small amount of memory on the CPU chip itself. This would be the various registers, and in later versions of the chip, some cache memory. Most of the primary memory is placed on the same circuit board as the cpu, and can be soldered in place, or can take the form of plug-in modules. This memory is random-access. Some of it will be persistent, read-only memory, but more will be read-write, volatile memory. Non-volatile memory retains its contents without applied power.

Computer memory is organized in a hierarchy. We would like to have large amounts of low-power, fast, non-volatile storage. These requirements are mutually exclusive. The memory closest to the CPU is fast, random-access, volatile, and semiconductor-based, but expensive. Secondary storage, such as disk or flash, is slower, cheaper, persistent, and cheaper on a cost-per-bit basis. Backup storage,, is still cheaper per bit, but may have a longer access time.

Other characteristics of interest include memory latency, the time it takes to access the requested item, and throughput, the read or write rate of the memory device. Some memory may have a relatively slow latency, but a very high throughput, once things get going.

The memory management unit (MMU) is an integral part of most processors, and maps virtual addresses to physical addresses. The virtual address space is much large than the physical space. There is an overhead involved with the mapping process, but having transparent access to a large amount of memory is usually an overriding advantage.

Virtual memory is an abstraction. We pretend we have more memory than is available in the system, but we only see a portion of this memory at a given time. The contents of the physical memory that we do have are managed by hardware, and are swapped in and out from secondary storage. Data is transferred in blocks. The program can be written without worrying about how much memory is available. Actually, if we add more physical memory, the systems will run faster, because fewer swaps are required.

Memory management allows a program to run anywhere in memory without being recompiled. It provides a level of protection and isolation between programs to prevent overwriting. It removes restrictions on the size of available memory by the virtual memory technique.

A memory management unit (MMU) translates memory addresses from logical/virtual to physical. This adds the overhead of translation to each memory access. In addition, the access time for the secondary storage may be a million times slower than for the primary memory, but it will have 100's of times large capacity, and certainly be cheaper. There is also the energy consumption issue.

When the CPU accesses a desired item, it may be present in the memory, or not. If not, the process generates a Page fault, resulting in an interrupt, with a request for data item not currently resident. This requires clever programming to be an efficient process. Too many misses, and the process bogs down in overhead.

The scheme requires data structures to keep track of what range of data addresses is actually present in memory, and registers or tables to allow arbitrary mappings of logical to physical addresses.

There are two basic schemes: segmented and paged. Paged usually deals with fixed sized blocks of memory, and segmentation is more flexible in terms of size. Segmentation and paging can be combined in certain architectures.

One application of memory mapping, often overlooked, is that the mapping process can map around failed physical memory, by moving pointers. It there is an active memory error detection and correction scheme running in hardware (or software), the mapping tables can be used to move code or data out of problem areas in the physical memory, without changing the associated program (or data) address.

Cache reduces the average access time for data, but will increase the worst-case time. The size and organization of the cache defines the performance for a given program. The proper size and organization is the subject of research.

Caches introduce indeterminacy into execution time. With cache, memory access time is no longer deterministic. We can't necessarily tell, a priori, if an item is or is not in cache. This can be a problem in real-time systems.

In multicore architectures, each CPU core may have its own L1 cache, but share L2 caches with other cores. Local data in the L1 caches must be consistent with data in other L1 caches. If one core changes a value in cache due to a write operation, that data needs to be changed in other caches as well (if they hold the same item). This is referred to as cache snooping, to retain consistency.

I/O

I/O involves getting data into and out of the cpu, or getting data from one point to another, via serial or parallel data busses. Communication interfaces in embedded systems, especially space systems, tend to be specialized, but can use industry-standard interfaces as well. The usual computer communications methods of polled I/O, interrupt-based I/O, and direct memory access are applicable. The data communication can be *serial* (bit at a time) or *parallel* (many bits at a time). There is an upper limit to the distance for parallel communications due to bit skew and cross-talk

Analog input and output is handled by digital to analog and analog to digital converters. Some embedded computer chips have these functions built in. Standard industry interfaces such as *USB* (Universal Serial Bus) are becoming standard in embedded systems as well. This provides access to a wide variety of devices, with no custom interfacing required. Serial I/O is bit-at-a-time, time-domain multiplexing of the signal.

Regardless how bits or signals come to a computer, there are several standards methods to sample them, or send them out. The various communication protocols define the physical connection (connectors) and electrical interface (voltages, etc.). Once we are at the processor chip boundary, and we are dealing with bits, there are three common schemes to read or write. These can be implemented in hardware or software. The three schemes are polled I/O, interrupts, or direct memory access. All of these schemes work with serial (bit-at-a-time) or parallel (many-bits-at-a-time) I/O.

In *polled I/O*, the computer periodically checks to see if data is available, or if the communications channel is ready to accept new output. This is somewhat like checking your phone every 5 seconds to see if anyone is calling. There's a more efficient way to do it, which we'll discuss next, but you may not have anything better to do. Polled I/O is the simplest method.

In *Interrupt I/O*, when a new piece of information arrives, or the communication channel is ready to accept new output, a control signal called an interrupt occurs. This is like the phone ringing. You are sitting at your desk, busy at something, and the phone rings, interrupting you, causing you to set aside what you are doing, and handle the new task. When that is done, you go back to what you were doing.

A special piece of software called an *interrupt service routine* is required. This is similar to a subroutine. The interrupt forces the next instruction to be a call to a predetermined location, the interrupt service routine. The return address is saved to resume executing the foreground program. You might jot down some notes to get back to what you were doing, when the phone call ends.

Direct Memory Access is the fastest way to input or output information. It does this directly to or from memory, without processor intervention or overhead. It is a way to block-move data in a rapid fashion, other than by cpu read followed by cpu write for each item.

Let's say we want to transmit a series of 32-bit words. The processor would have to fetch each word from memory, send it to the I/O interface, and update a counter. In DMA, the I/O device can interface directly to or from the memory. DMA control hardware includes housekeeping tasks such as maintaining the word count, and updating the memory pointer.

DMA can also make use of interrupts. Normally, we load a word count into a register in the DMA controller, and it is counted down as words transfer to or from memory. When the word count reaches zero, an interrupt is triggered to the processor to signal the end of the transfer event.

While the DMA is going on, the processor may be locked out of memory access, depending on the memory architecture. Also, if dynamic memory is being used, the processor is usually in charge of memory refresh. This can be also be handled by the DMA controller, but someone has to do it.

One DMA scheme, used on the IBM pc, toggles between the CPU and the DMA device on a per-word basis. Thus, the processor is never locked out of fetching and executing instructions during a DMA for more than 1 cycle, although the DMA operation is not as fast as it could be.

Also, DMA is not constrained to access memory linearly; that is a function of the DMA controller and its complexity. For example, the DMA controller might be set up to access every fourth word in memory, and data items can be reordered in memory to facilitate processing. This is used in certain digital signal processing schemes. The DMA controller may also support complete re-ordering of the data words.

The DMA protocol uses a *Request and Grant mechanism*. The device desiring to use dma send a request to the cpu, and that request is granted

36

when the cpu is able. This is similar to the interrupt request for service mechanism. A dma controller interfaces with the device and the cpu. It may handle multiple dma channels with differing priorities. The controller has to know, for each request, the starting address in memory, and the size of the data movement. For dma data coming in to ram, there may be the additional complication of updating cache.

During the dma transfer, the dma controller takes over certain tasks form the cpu. This includes updating the memory address, and keeping track of the word count. The word count normally goes to zero, and generates an interrupt to signal the cpu that the dma transfer is over. The cpu can continue execution, as long as it has code and data available.

DMA in multicore systems is more exciting. In multicore, dma between the caches can be used as an inter-processor communication mechanism, and cache-cache transfers are supported. There is a cache coherency protocol between the various caches. It is the responsibility of the operating system to enforce this protocol, although hardware mechanisms (like the I/O coherent ARM Cortex A9) are appearing. This is usually implemented with a snooping mechanism, facilitated by hardware. A common cache coherency protocol is termed MESI, standing for Modified, Exclusive, Shared, and Invalid, referring to the possible states of each cache line.

DMA support is the responsibility of the operating system, and modern operating systems handle the complexities of multi-dma in multicore systems.

Onboard interfaces

A bus *architecture* is used as a short-distance communications pathway between functional elements, such as the cpu and memory. Busses can be serial or parallel. The length of parallel signal lines is severely restricted by bit skew, where all the bits don't necessarily get to a particular point at the same time. This is due in some part by the differing characteristics of the parallel wires or traces implementing the bus. Each path must be treated as a transmission line at the frequencies involved, must have balanced characteristics with all the other lines, and be properly terminated. We'll discuss some common I/O interfaces used in embedded, particularly space systems.

PCI Express

PCI Express is a serial bus that replaced standard pci and the specialized AGP bus. The PCI special Interest group (PCI-SIG) is an industry group of some 900 companies. It is the bus architecture of choice for current desktops, laptops, and servers. It is a point-point system that uses packets used for data. Besides its use on motherboards, it can be extended with cabling.

I²C

The *Inter-Integrated Circuit* (I²C) bus is designed for short-range communication between chips on a board. It is a 2-wire interface that is multi-master, and bidirectional. There are 7-bit slave addresses, so 128 unique devices can be addressed from the current master. It was developed by Philips Semiconductor in the 1980's, and is widely used in embedded systems.

SPI/Microwire

The *Serial Peripheral Interface* (SPI) bus is a full-duplex synchronous serial communication system. It is a master/slave architecture. It uses four wires for the serial clock, the master-in/slave-out, the master-out/slave-in, and a slave-select. It is the basis for the *JTAG* (Joint Test Action Group)'s diagnostic interface, and has found application in general I/O device interfacing as well. Microwire is a SPI predecessor, that is half-duplex.

CAN

The *Controller Area Network* (CAN) dates from 1983, and has its origins in industrial control and automation. It was developed by Robert Bosch GmbH in 1986, has been widely used in the automotive industry. It has a message-based protocol, and is a multi-master broadcast serial bus. The theoretical limit for devices on the bus is over 2,000, but a practical limit is about 100. It is a two-wire, half-duplex arrangement. It operates at a conservative 1 mbps, and has error detection and containment features. It is widely used in embedded systems and space applications. It is a proprietary standard.

RS-422/423

These are ANSI and international standards. They use a balanced voltage, or differential scheme. They can be implemented in a multi-drop or point-point architecture. The standards are for the electrical signaling only. RS-423 uses unbalanced signaling at 4 Mbps, over twisted pair.

These communication schemes use differential drivers over a 2-wire link. Common ground reduces the effect of external noise and cable effects. Voltage swings can be minimized, (faster transmission and less cross-talk) and less susceptible to voltage differences between the grounds of transmitter and receiver.

RS-485 is an enhanced RS-422. There can be 32 drivers and 32 receivers on a bi-directional bus. The line typically terminated at the ends by resistors. Addressing uses a polled master/slave protocol.

Spacewire

Spacewire is IEEE standard 1355. It was developed at the European Space Agency (ESA), and represents a full-duplex, point-to-point routable protocol. A routable protocol has both a network address and a device address. I can forward packets from on network to another. TCP/IP is a routable protocol.

Spacewire operates to 400 megabits per second. Space-rated radiation tolerant parts are available, as are IP cores. A new standard called SpaceFibre is emerging for higher data rates, and routable protocols.

MIL-STD-1553

MIL-STD-1553 is a digital time division multiplexed command/response multiplex avionics bus, used in aircraft and spacecraft, dating from 1973. It uses a coax cable medium, and Manchester bi-phase encoding for code and data transmission. There is a bus controller (BC) and remote terminals (RT's). RT-RT data transmission is allowed, under control for the Bus Controller master. 1553 uses 16-bit words, at a rate of 1 megabit per second. A follow-on standard, 1773, extends the data transmission rate, and uses optical fiber media.

Software bus

The term software bus refers to a mechanism that allows modules or processes to exchange information without worrying about the details of the underlying hardware. It is a virtual bus, with the functionality implemented in software.

Uplink and downlink

Uplink refers to data sent to the spacecraft, and downlink refers to data sent by the spacecraft. These can travel by radio frequency or light.

Protocols

The CCSDS, Consultive Committee on Space Data Standards, has a series of International standards for space data systems. There are eleven member nations as members. They publish standards in six major areas of interest, including spacecraft onboard interfaces. Other standards cover systems engineering, space link, and space inter-networking. On their web site, they list 750 missions using their defined protocols.

TCP/IP protocols

The Transmission Control Protocol and the Internet Protocol enable our world wide, and solar-system wide digital communications infrastructure. TCP/IP enables end-end connectivity and data delivery. There are four layers in the scheme, the link, the internet, the transport, and the application layers. Most of the work on TCP/IP came from Vint Cerf's work at Stanford University for DARPA. There is a vast library of TCP/IP standards and best practices. Two of the key architectural principals are defined in the architectural document RFC 1122. The RFC, or Request for Comment, is the mechanism for reviewing documents by the user community. RFC 1132 defines the end-to-end principle, and the robustness principal.

The end-to-end principle has evolved since its expression put the maintenance of state and overall intelligence at the edges, and assumed the Internet that connected the edges retained no state and concentrated on speed and simplicity. Real-world needs for firewalls, network address translators, web content caches and the like have forced evolutionary changes in this principle. The Robustness principle says "In general, an implementation must be conservative in its sending behavior, and liberal in its receiving behavior. That is, it must be careful to send well-formed datagrams, but must accept any datagram that it can interpret." The second part of the principle is almost as important: software on other hosts may contain deficiencies that make it unwise to exploit legal but obscure protocol features." These two principles have driven the implementation of the Internet we use today, on Earth, and between the planets. TCP/IP defines abstraction layers for network topology and data flow among systems. A complete discussion of TCP/IP is beyond the scope of this book, but is an important topic in understanding how and why modern data communications works the way it does.

IP-in-space

The use of Internet Protocol for space missions is a convenience, and piggy-backs on the large established infrastructure of terrestrial data traffic. However, there are problems. A variation of mobile IP is used, because the spacecraft might not always be in view of a ground station, and traffic through the Tracking and Data Relay Satellites involves a significant delay. A hand-off scheme between various "cell" sites must be used, and a delay-tolerant protocol. However, onboard the spacecraft, the CISCO CLEO router may be used, to route onboard IP traffic.

Cubesat Space Protocol

This is a network layer protocol, specifically for Cubesats, released in 2010 It features a 32-bit header with both network layer and transport layer data. It is written in the c language, and works with linux and FreeRTOS. The protocol and its implementation is Open source. At the physical layer, the protocol supports CAN bus, I2C, RS-232, TCP/IP, and CCDSDS space link protocol.

Interplanetary Internet

Communications between planets in our solar system involves long distances, and significant delay. New protocols are needed to address the long delay times, and error sources.

A concept called the Interplanetary Internet uses a store-and-forward node in orbit around a planet (initially, Mars) that would burst-transmit data back to Earth during available communications windows. At certain times, when the geometry is right, the Mars bound traffic might encounter significant interference. Mars surface craft communicate to Orbiters, which relay the transmissions to Earth. This allows for a lower wattage transmitter on the surface vehicle. Mars does not (yet) have the full infrastructure that is currently in place around the Earth – a network of navigation, weather, and communications satellites.

For satellites in near Earth orbit, protocols based on the cellular terrestrial network can be used, because the delays are small. In fact, the International

Space Station is a node on the Internet. By the time you get to the moon, it takes about a second and a quarter for electromagnetic energy to traverse the distance. Delay tolerant protocols were developed for mobile terrestrial communication, but break down in very long delay situations.

We have a good communications model and a lot of experience in Internet communications. One of the first implementations for space used a File Transfer Protocol (FPP) running over CCSDS space communications protocol in 1996.

The formalized Interplanetary Internet evolved from a study at JPL, lead by Internet pioneer Vint Cerf, and Adrian Hook, from the CCSDS group. The concepts evolved to address very long delay and variable delay in communications links. For example, the Earth to Mars delay varies depending on where each planet is located in its orbit around the Sun. For some periods, one planet is behind the Sun from the point of view of the other, and communications between them is impossible for days and weeks.

The Interplanetary Internet implements a Bundle Protocol to address large and variable delays. Normal IP traffic assumes a seamless, end-to-end, available data path, without worrying about the physical mechanism. The Bundle protocol addresses the case of high probability of errors, and disconnections. This protocol was tested in communication with an Earth orbiting satellite in 2008

Sensors and sensor interfacing

A *sensor* is a device that measures a physical quantity by changing state in response to the stimulation, and producing a signal. It is an analog world. It is rare that we get to interface directly to a digital source. Some sensors may indicate one of two states (presence/absence) with a simple digital signal that may only require voltage level shifting. Other signals, such as a switch closure, may appear digital, but require *debouncing* due to the physics of the actual contact, which actually closes and opens hundreds of times on activation. This is a form of signal conditioning for the sensor. We haven't yet considered voltage levels, current requirements, timing, and all those other real-world interfacing issues. We tend to view sensors as a "black-box" function, where the output is a valid representation of the applied signal. The ugly truth is, sensors are real-world devices that have their own non-linearity, parametric shifts, and they tend to respond to a lot more than the parameter we are interested in.

Some sensors output a digital value that could be sign-magnitude format, 1's complement, 2's complement, Grey code, or some other scheme. The data format might be BCD or binary (signed or unsigned) or something else. The word length may be unique to the sensor, and the data may not come out all at the same time – it might be serial by bit, serial by byte, MSB first, LSB first, etc.

Passive sensors simply collect energy from the sensed phenomena; active sensors require power, or an excitation signal. A *transducer* is a device that converts one form of energy to another; a solar cell is an example. In the literature, the terms sensor and transducer are often used interchangeably.

All sensors are built to operate within a specified environment that corresponds to the temperature limits and other environmental conditions of its applied surroundings. Even if other sensors exist, they may not satisfy all essential conditions to operate within the system, including operating life, sensing range, accuracy, redundancy, low energy consumption, environments, mounting mechanism, reliability, sensing rate with response time, volume, and mass.

It is expected that the software in the embedded processor will sort this all out. With Smart Sensors with integrated processing, more common interface standards between the sensor and the main processor can be applied.

Signal conditioning refers to processing the sensed signal into a form from which the digital processor can then extract useful information. This may involve amplification or attenuation, analog to digital conversion, filtering, format conversion, electrical isolation, and other techniques. Noise filtering is a commonly applied technique. Sensors exhibit lag and hysteresis, which is a difference in offset from one measurement direction to another. Bias refers to the situation when the output is not zero when the measured quantity is. There can be dynamic errors, caused by rapid change in the input. *Drift* refers to the fact that, over time, the sensor changes output while the input remains steady.

The physics of the sensor must be considered. A relative humidity sensor measures relative humidity, but also temperature. A digital compass also reacts to magnetic fields produced by nearby wiring. Sensors are inherently non-linear. All of these characteristics must be understood and compensated for in software or hardware. With smart sensors, this compensation and processing would be accomplished within the sensor unit itself. For a simple sensor unit, some processing and conditioning must be done within the main embedded processor. Consider issues of operating life, range, maximum and minimum, accuracy, redundancy, energy consumption, heat generation, electromagnetic interference generation, electromagnetic interference susceptibility, mounting, reliability, sense rate, transient and steady-state response time, mass and volume, aging, and mean time to failure when choosing sensors.

As an example, the output signal may not vary linearly with the sensed value, and may depend on other ambient conditions as well. A polynomial function in software may need to be applied to the sensed input to generate the correct output. This can be implemented by calculation, or a table look-up.

Between the sensor and the processor, we may need a level of isolation, to protect either or both sides. This might be optical, capacitive, or magnetic in nature. Common grounding is also a concern.

There are specialized sensors all over the spacecraft, both for housekeeping, navigation, and operations, but also on the payload side for science data acquisition. In a lot of cases, the instrument is purpose built for a particular mission, and is the first of its kind. Science instruments can produce huge data volumes that must be ingested, archived, and transmitted to the ground.

Attitude control sensors include sun sensors, Horizon sensors, magnetometers, star sensors. There is a large collection of inexpensive, commercial grade MEMS units such as gyros, IR and UV sensors, thermal sensors, acceleration sensors available. Most of these interface via i2c bus.

Accelerometers

Accelerometers use a known proof mass and a force sensor. The typical unit would have three sensors in quadrature to give an X-Y-Z reading. Accelerometers implemented in MEMS technology involve a small proof mass that bends a silicon beam, and the deflection is measured by a built-in strain gage.

Gyros

A *gyroscope* is a device for measuring or maintaining orientation, based on the principles of angular momentum. Mechanically, a gyroscope is a spinning wheel or disk in which the axle is free to assume any orientation. Although this orientation does not remain fixed, it changes in response to an external torque much less and in a different direction than it would without the large angular momentum associated with the disk's high rate of spin and moment of inertia. Since external torque is minimized by mounting the device in gimbals, its orientation remains nearly fixed, regardless of any motion of the platform on which it is mounted. The force at the gimbals can be measured with strain gages. An electric motor, or an air motor maintains the gyroscope's rotation rate.

Gyroscopes can also be electronic, microchip-packaged MEMS devices that are commonly found in consumer electronic devices such as cell phones and video games, solid-state ring lasers, or fiber optics. These do not use a rotating mass.

Applications of gyroscopes include inertial navigation systems where magnetic compasses would not work or would not be precise enough, and for stabilization.

The problem with gyros is their drift with time. The gyro's advantage is continuous output and they are not constrained by the need for an external reference.

Sun Sensors

Sun sensors are universally applied to spacecraft. At least around Earth, the Sun is significantly bright to distinguish it from any other celestial object. Out in the outer planets, the Sun is less distinctive. Knowing where the Sun is located relative to the spacecraft is essential for proper orientation of the solar panels, to ensure a flow of charging current to the batteries. It is also a good rough orientation and orbital positing tool. Eclipses of the sun with respect to the spacecraft can be confusing unless anticipated.

Earth Sensor

An Earth sensor, or horizon sensor, can see the interface between cool space, and the warm Earth. This is usually done in the infrared spectrum. Generically, you can use a horizon sensor for a spacecraft in orbit around any planet. Horizon sensors can be sometimes disrupted by the Sun, if it is in the field of view. . The relative size of the planetary images give a rough value of the satellite's altitude.

For a satellite in Earth orbit, if the moon is visible to the side of the Earth, it interferes with the image. The same is true around other planets with moons.

Star Sensors

Star sensors measure star coordinates in a spacecraft frame of reference and provide attitude information when these observed coordinates are compared with known star directions obtained from a star catalog (data base). Star sensors can achieve accuracies in the arc-second range. Most star sensors consist of a Sunshade, an optical system, an image definition device which defines the region of the field of view that is visible to the detector, the detector and an electronic assembly. The detector such as a photomultiplier transforms the optical signal into an electrical signal. Solid-state detectors may be noisier than photomultipliers. The electronics assembly amplifies and filters the electrical signal from the detector. If the amplified optical signal from the detector is above a fixed signal intensity, an output is generated signifying the star's presence.

A charge transfer device star sensor is an optical system consisting of a digitally scanned array of photosensitive elements whose output is fed to an embedded microprocessor. A charge pattern corresponding to the received image of the star field viewed is produced, and is stored in memory for later processing.

The star sensor data is applied to a table of known stars. These "fixed" stars can be used for position and attitude information. Brightness is also used to verify the star identity. The star table is generally in celestial coordinates, and the observation is made from a known body-fixed position of the star sensor on the spacecraft.

Magnetometers

Magnetometers measure the induced current in a coil by a planet's magnetic field. This works well at Earth, where the magnetic field has been well mapped. For planets with little or no magnetic field, such as Mars, magnetometers are not very useful. A more sensitive measurement is made with a fluxgate. A fluxgate magnetometer consists of a small, magnetically susceptible core wrapped by two coils of wire. An alternating electric current is passed through one coil, driving the core through an alternating cycle of magnetic saturation. This constantly changing field induces an electric current in the second coil, and this output current is measured by a detector. In a magnetically neutral background, the input and output currents will match. When the core is exposed to a background magnetic field, it will be more easily saturated in alignment with that field and less easily saturated in opposition to it. The induced output current, will be out of step with the input current. The extent to which this happens depends on the strength of the magnetic field.

The normal spacecraft residual magnetism, and generated electromagnetic fields form the operation of electrical equipment interfere with the sensitive magnetometers.

GPS

The GPS in-orbit satellite-based navigation can be used by satellites below the GPS spacecraft orbit (at 12,600 miles) for time and position services. Generally, four GPS satellites must be in view simultaneously. Commercial off-the-shelf rad-hard gps products for spacecraft are available. This, of course, assumes the planter you are in orbit about has a constellation of GPS satellites. Only Earth, so far.

Actuators

It is an analog world. Until recently, a digital interface to a motor or actuator was not common. Digital to analog conversion circuits were required. The other issue is power amplification. The actuators usually operate beyond the available range of voltages of computer components, and may require orders of magnitude more current. An actuator as we use the term here means an electrical to mechanical transducer. This includes motors and solenoids.

Attitude control can take the form of reaction wheels, where a small mass is spun rapidly, and the large structure of the spacecraft moves in the opposite direction, preserving momentum. Reaction wheels use electrical motors. One problems occurs when there are biases that cause the reaction wheel to saturate in one direction. It must then be unloaded of momentum by reaction jet firing (involving electrically controlled valves), or torquer bars, which, when energized, push against the planet's magnetic field. Electric propulsion, or pulsed plasma propulsion can also be used to make attitude and orbit correction.

Gas jets can use a cold-gas source such as nitrogen, or a hot gas system with a propellant and oxidizer. The flow is controlled by solenoid valves, driven from the computer. Generally, accelerometers and gyros monitor the jet firing to see if the desired effect has been achieved. If not, a second firing can be used to the the results closer to the desired.

Spacecraft housekeeping Tasks

Besides attitude determination and control, the onboard embedded systems has a variety of housekeeping tasks to attend to.

Generally, there is a dedicated unit, sometimes referred to as the Command & Data Handler (C&DH) with interfaces with the spacecraft transmitters and receivers, the onboard data system, and the flight computer. The C&DH, itself a computer, is in charge of uplinked data (generally, commands), onboard data storage, and data transmission. The C&DH can send received commands directly to various spacecraft components, or can hold them for later dissemination at a specified time. The C&DH has a direct connection with the science instrument(s) for that data stream. If the science instrument package has multiple sensors, there may be a separate science C&DH (SC&DH) that consolidates the sensed data, and hands it over to the C&DH for transmission to the ground. It is also common for the C&DH to hand over all commands related to science instruments to the IC&DH.

Consumables inventory

The spacecraft computer calculates and maintains a table of consumables data, both value and usage rate. This includes available electrical power in the batteries, state-of-charge, the amount of thruster propellant remaining, and the status of any other renewable or consumable asset. This is periodically telemetered to the ground. Over the long term, we can do trending on this data, which can help us identify pending problems.

Thermal management

The spacecraft electronics needs to be kept within a certain temperature for proper operation. Generally, the only heat source is the Sun, and the only heat sink is deep space. There are options as to how the spacecraft can be oriented. In close orbit to a planet, the planet may also represent a heat source. Automatic thermal louvers can be used to regulate the spacecraft internal temperature, if they are pointed to deep space. The flight computer's job is to keep the science instrument or communications antennae pointed in the right direction. This might be overridden in case the spacecraft is getting too hot or too cold.

Electrical Power/energy management

The Flight Computer needs to know the state-of-charge (SOC) of the batteries at all times, and whether current is flowing into or out of the batteries. It the SOC is getting too low, some operations must be suspended, so the solar panels or spacecraft itself can be re-oriented to maximize charging. In some cases, redundant equipment may be turned off, according to a predetermined load-shedding algorithm. If the spacecraft batteries are fully discharged, it is generally the end of the mission, because pointing to the Sun cannot be achieved, except by lucky accident. Don't bet on it.

Antenna Pointing

The spacecraft communications antennae must be pointed to the large antennae on the ground (Earth) or to a communications relay satellite in a higher orbit (for Earth or Mars). The Antennae can usually be steered in two axis, independently of the spacecraft body. This can be accomplished in the Main flight computer, or be a task for the C&DH.

Safe Hold mode

As a last resort, the spacecraft has a safe-hold or survival mode that operates without computer intervention. This usually seeks to orient the spacecraft with its solar panels to the Sun to maximize power, turn off all non-essential systems, and call for help. This can be implemented in a dedicated digital unit. It used to be the case that the safe-hold mode was implemented in analog circuitry.

Special requirements for Rovers

A spacecraft on the surface of another planet is designed to move around. We can envision similar units that fly or dive under extra-terrestrial oceans, but these haven't been implemented yet. A balloon-borne payload or Aerostat is also feasible.

We have launched the most landing platforms to the moon, but have the most experience with Rovers on Mars. Generally, the landing platform serves as a communication relay, and a small rover is directed to explore. Recently, larger platforms have had the ability to communication via the increasingly complex Mars orbital infrastructure, which includes weather satellites and communication relays to Earth.

The Soviet Union launched a series of successful lunar landers, sample return missions, and lunar rovers. The Lunokhod missions, from 1969 through 1977, put a series of remotely controlled vehicles on the lunar surface. Lunokhod-1 was an 8-wheeled rover, operated from Earth. It was the first Rover to land on a body other than Earth. It deployed from the landing platform via a ramp. It was operational for 11 months. The follow-on Lunokhod-2 Rover could transmit live video from the surface, and had a series of soil property instruments. Its tracks were seen by the Lunar Reconnaissance Orbiter in 2010. The first and second rovers remain on the moon, although the second rover was sold in 1993 at a Southby's auction. The buyer was Richard Garriott, son of Astronaut Owen Garriott. As of this writing, he has not picked up his property.

The initial purpose for the Lunokhod series was to scout sites for manned landings, and to serve as beacons. The rover could be used to move one Cosmonaut at a time on the surface as well. Lunokhod had a group of four television cameras, and mechanical mechanisms to test the lunar soil. There was also an X-ray fluorescence spectrometer, and a cosmic ray detector. The second unit conducted laser ranging experiments from Earth via a corner reflector, and measured local magnetic fields. The rover was driven by a team on Earth in teleoperation mode. This is just at the edge of feasible, given the delay in communications due to the distance.

The NASA Surveyor missions of 1966-68 landed seven spacecraft on the surface of the moon, as preparation for the Apollo manned missions. Five of these were soft landings, as intended. All of these were fixed instrument platforms. Interestingly, Apollo-12 astronauts landed near Surveyor 3, and returned with some pieces. Not just souvenirs, these were used to evaluate the long term exposure of materials on the lunar surface.

Yutu is the name of the Chinese Lunar Rover, and means Jade Rabbit. It was launched in December of 2013. It landed successfully on the moon, but became stationary after the second lunar night. It is a 300 pound vehicle with a selection of science instruments, including an infrared spectrometer, 4 mast-mounted cameras including a video camera, and an alpha particle x-ray spectrometer. The rover is equipped with an arm. It also carries a ground penetrating radar. It is designed to enter hibernation mode during the 2-week lunar night. It does post status updates to the Internet, and still serves as a stationary sensor platform.

Robot explorers on Earth

We can think of these as Earth satellites at zero altitude. NASA sponsored the Robotics Institute at Carnegie Mellon University to build the Nomad Rover, a 4-wheeled, 1,600 pound autonomous explorer. It was deployed in Antarctica in the year 2000. It's job is to find meteorites. It turns out, a lot of the meteorites found in Antarctica are from Mars, based on chemical composition. Nomad is doing the a similar job on Earth that the Mars Rovers are doing on Mars.

Nomad is equipped with a laser rangefinder, high resolution cameras, onboard computer, satellite data link, and a gasoline-powered generator. It is looking for meteorites on the ice with a specific set of characteristics. If one is detected, it navigates to the target for a closer look. It has an arm with a camera and spectrometer, as well as a metal detector. If the rock meets the profile of being a potential meteorite, the GPS location is logged. The robot does not collect samples, but does sort through rock fields for items of interest.

A rock the size of a potato (Allan Hills 84001) found in Antarctica in 1984 definitely came from Mars, and had chemical and fossil evidence of life. It is yet to be proven whether this definitely shows the past presence of life on Mars.

Power Concerns, and the Cost of Computation

Generally, the computer hardware can be designed to minimize the amount of power it consumes. The next issue is to control the amount of power the software takes.

Power is a constrained resource onboard the spacecraft, and must be carefully managed. We generally have rechargeable batteries, and solar arrays for a power source. The computer has to monitor and control the state-of-charge of the batteries, sometimes dropping everything it is doing to charge the batteries.

We also have to consider the power usage of the computer, while executing programs. Most embedded systems have some power saving modes, that come in handy for your cellphone, for example. These modes have names like "sleep" and "standby." The manufacturers' data sheet will define these modes, and their power consumption, compared to normal operation. In addition, some computers can selectively shut down some memory or I/O resources to reduce power as well.

To control power usage, we first need to add instrumentation to measure it. The embedded processor needs to be able to monitor its own power consumption. On the test bench, we can establish the energy required to run an algorithm. From this data, we make decisions according to the current situation and state as to the correct approach to apply. What we have measured and computed is the energy cost of computation.

Let's look at a simple example of onboard data processing on a small satellite imaging mission. Here we are taking consecutive images at a resolution of 5 megapixels. This is 40 megabits, at 8 bits per pixel. In Cubesats, you have a limited downlink bandwidth due to power issues, and you only have communications over land. Cubesat generally do not have the resources to utilize the Tracking and Data Relay Satellites at a higher orbit. This implies we need to know when we are over land. There are lots of ways to do this, but we could run a simple orbit model onboard with stored maps. The spacecraft takes images continuously, stores them onboard, and downlinks them when a receiver is available.

We could also consider doing some image processing onboard. The Raspberry Pi, Model B 2, for example has an Image Processing pipeline separate from the main cpu cores. It is supported by an open source image processing library. We can implement various levels of data compressing on the image, or do image differencing, or process to only include "areas of interest." All of this is feasible, but involves a lot of computation, which, in turn, uses a lot of power. So, we might consider only doing the computations, on stored data, when the cubesat is in sunlight. Again, we can predict this, and it is relatively easy to sense.

We might run into a conflict between processing the images, and downlinking them, if the cubesat is in sunlight, and over land. A housekeeping task for an onboard computer is to keep track of the state-of-charge of the battery's by measuring current in and current out.

Self Monitoring Systems

Homeostasis refers to a system that monitors, corrects, and controls its own state. Our bodies do that with our blood pressure, temperature, blood auger level, and many other parameters.

We can have the embedded processor monitor its performance, or have two identical systems monitor each other. Each approach has problems. We can also choose to "triplicate" the hardware, and use external logic to see if results differ. The idea is, two outweigh one, because the probability of a double error is less than that of a single error.

In at least one case I know of, the backup computer erroneously thought the primary machine made a mistake, and took over control. It was wrong, and caused a system failure.

To counter the effects of "bit flips" and other effects of radiation, the memory can be designed with error detection and correction (EDAC). Generally, this means a longer, encoded word that can detect n and correct M errors. There is a trade-off with price. With EDAC memory, there is a low priority background task running on the cpu that continuously reading and writing back to memory. This process, called "memory scrubbing" will catch and correct errors.

Self-test software can be included, usually running as a background task. This might also send a "heart-beat" signal to another processor or logic. At the hardware level, particularly if we are using configurable logic, we can include built-in self test (BIST).

A special-purpose timer essential for embedded applications is the Watchdog. This is a free-running timer that generates a cpu reset unless it is reset by the software. This helps to ensure that the system doesn't lock up during certain critical time periods, and the software is meeting its deadlines. This approach has saved many a system.

If the watchdog is not reset, it generates an interrupt to reset the host. This should take the system back to a baseline state, and restart it. Hopefully, normal operations will resume. The embedded system can't rely on a human operator to notice a fault in the operations or a "hung" system, and press the reset button. Many *very remote* systems, such as those in deep water or on the surface of other planets have successfully recovered from faults with a watchdog.

The watchdog timer is implemented in hardware, and does it's jobs without direct software intervention. If the software fails to reset the timer, the system reboots. This might simply reset operations and restart, or may include diagnostics before the system is restarted. So, who watches the watchdog?

Flight Software

This section discusses the software that runs on the spacecraft flight computers. It provides provides the ground system with an interface to the flight hardware. Some parts are rarely changed from mission to mission, like the implementation of communication protocols. Other elements, particularly supporting the payloads, are fairly unique for each mission.

The flight software has to respond to onboard events that the ground systems cannot. This may be because of communications delays, or loss of contact. It is the flight software running on the flight computer that is there, on the spot. It has a global view of the state of onboard systems. At the same time, downlink bandwidth is limited, and there is a trade-off between downlink, and onboard processing. One of the key tasks of the onboard system is the health and safety of the spacecraft, and mission continuity.

Open Source vs Proprietary

This is a topic we need to discuss before we get very far into software. It is not a technical topic, but concerns your right to use (and/or own, modify) software. It's those software licenses you click to agree with, and never read. That's what the intellectual property lawyers are betting on.

Software and software tools are available in proprietary and open source versions. Open source software is free and widely available, and may be incorporated into your system. It is available under license, which generally says that you can use it, but derivative products must be made available under the same license. This presents a problem if it is mixed with purchased, licensed commercial software, or a level of exclusivity is required. Major government agencies such as the Department of Defense and NASA have policies related to the use of Open Source software.

Adapting a commercial or open source operating system to a particular problem domain can be tricky. Usually, the commercial operating systems need to be used "as-is" and the source code is not available. The software can usually be configured between well-defined limits, but there will be no visibility of the internal workings. For the open source situation, there will be a multitude of source code modules and libraries that can be configured and customized, but the process is complex. The user can also write new modules in this case.

Large corporations or government agencies sometimes have problems incorporating open source products into their projects. Open Source did not fit the model of how they have done business traditionally. They are issues and lingering doubts. Many Federal agencies have developed Open Source policies. NASA has created an open source license, the NASA Open Source Agreement (NOSA), to address these issues.

It has released software under this license, but the Free Software Foundation had some issues with the terms of the license. The Open Source Initiative (OpenSource.org) maintains the definition of Open Source, and certifies licenses such as the NOSA. (HTTP://opensource.org/licenses/NASA-1.3) The GNU General Public License (GPL) is the most widely used free software license. It guarantees end users the freedoms to use, study, share, copy, and modify the software. Software that ensures that these rights are retained is called free software. The license was originally written by Richard Stallman of the Free Software Foundation (FSF) for the GNU project in 1989. The GPL is a *copyleft* license, which means that derived works can only be distributed under the same license terms. This is in distinction to permissive free software licenses, of which the BSD licenses are the standard examples. Copyleft is in counterpoint to traditional copyright. Proprietary software "poisons" free software, and cannot be included or integrated with it, without abandoned the GPL. The GPL covers the GNU/linux operating systems and most of the GNU/linux-based applications.

A Vendor's software tools and operating system or application code is usually proprietary intellectual property. It is unusual to get the source code to examine, at least without binding legal documents and additional funds. Along with this, you do get the vendor support. An alternative is open source code, which is in the public domain. There are a series of licenses covering open source code usage, including the Creative Commons License, the gnu public license, copyleft, and others. Open Source describes a collaborative environment for development and testing. Use of open source code carries with it an implied responsibility to "pay back" to the community. Open Source is not necessarily free.

The Open source philosophy is sometimes at odds with the rigidized procedures evolved to ensure software performance and reliability. Offsetting this is the increased visibility into the internals of the software packages, and control over the entire software package. Besides application code, operating systems such as GNU/linux and bsd can be open source. The programming language Python is open source. The popular web server Apache is also open source.

Operating Systems

An *operating system* (OS) is a software program that manages computer hardware and software resources, and provides common services for execution of various application programs. Without an operating system, a user cannot run an application program on their computer, unless the application program is itself self-booting.

For hardware functions such as input, output, and memory allocation, the operating system acts as an intermediary between application programs and the computer hardware, although the application code is usually executed directly by the hardware and will frequently call the OS or be interrupted by it. Operating systems are found on almost any device that contains a computer. The operating system functions need to be addressed by software (or possibly hardware), even if there is no entity that we can point to, called the Operating System. In simple, usually single-task programs, there might not be an operating system per se, but the functionality is still part of the overall software.

An operating system manages computer resources, including:
- Memory.
- I/O.
- Interrupts.
- Tasks/processes/application programs.
- File system
- clock time.

The operating system arbitrates and enforces priorities. If there are not multiple software entities to arbitrate among, the job is simpler. An operating system can be off-the-shelf commercial or open source code, or the application software developer can decide to build his or her own. To avoid unnecessary reinvention of the wheel an available product is usually chosen.

Operating systems are usually large and complex pieces of software. This is because they have to be generic in function, as the originator does not know what application space it will be used in. Operating systems for desktop/network/server application are usually not applicable for embedded applications. Mostly they are too large, having many components that will not be needed (such as the human interface), and they do not address the real-time requirements of the embedded domain.

Adapting a commercial or open source operating system to a particular embedded domain can be tricky. Usually, the commercial operating systems need to be used "as-is" and the source code is not available. The software can usually be configured between well-defined limits, but there will be no visibility of the internal workings. For the open source situation, there will be a multitude of source code modules and libraries that can be configured and customized, but the process is complex. The user can also write new modules in this case.

Operating Systems designed for the desktop are well suited for embedded There were developed under the assumption that whatever memory is required will be available, and real-time operation with hard deadlines is not required.

Real-time operating systems, as opposed to those addressing desktop, tablet, and server applications, emphasize predictability and consistency rather than throughput and low latencies. Determinism is probably the most important feature in a real-time operating system.

A microkernel operating system is ideally suited to embedded systems. It is slimmed down to include only those features needed, with no additional code. Barebones is the term sometimes used. The microkernel handles memory management, threads, and communication between processes. It has device drivers for only those devices present. The operating systems may have to be recompiled when new devices are added. A file system, if required, is run in user space. MINIX, as an example of a streamlined kernel, with about 6,000 lines of code.

File Systems

Use of an industry-standard file system will ease the interface to ground based storage and processing. There are several popular file systems, usually defined as part of a specific operating system. A file system provides a way to organized your data, and file systems management services are part of the operating system. The operating systems may support several file formats. A file system organizes data. It presents a data-centric view of a digital storage system.

A file is a container of information, usually stored as a one-dimensional array of bytes. Historically, the file format and the nature of the file system were driven by the mechanism of data storage. On early computer tape units for mainframes, the access mechanism was serial, leading to long access times. With disk and solid-state storage, the access time is vastly improved, as the device is random access – the same access time applies for any data item.

Metadata includes information about the data in a file. This consists of the file name and type, and other parameters such as the size, date and time of creation, the data and time of last access, the owner and read/write/access permissions, when a backup was last made, and other related information.

A directory, like the manila file folder, is a special file that points to ("contains") other files. This allows files to be organized, and implements a hierarchical file system.

There are many file system standards. The Microsoft operating systems support the FAT and NTFS file systems among others. The FAT (File Allocation System) format originated with early support of 8-bit microprocessor systems with MS-DOS. Fat-12 and FAT-16 had restrictions on the number of files in the root file system, but this has largely been removed with the introduction of FAT-32. File names are restricted to 8 characters, with a 3-character type specifier, the 8.3 format for file names. NTFS is the extended file system developed for the Windows-NT and subsequent operating systems from Microsoft. Linux supports a variety of file formats, including ext2, ext3, and ext4. There are plenty of choices; don't re-invent the wheel.

Real-time programming and design

Programming for real-time systems involves a few more details to keep track of. The same application of the system design process applies, but we need to keep in mind the overwhelming new requirement of real-time operation, where the right answer, late, is wrong. We'll look at how to identify and analyze the timing requirements for real-time systems.

Real time systems can be categorized as hard real time and soft real time. In hard real time systems, critical pieces have absolute deadlines, and missing deadline means system failure. The response times must be deterministic. In soft real time systems, the average performance or response time is emphasized and missing a deadline is not necessarily catastrophic. Predictability of the system behavior is required.

Soft real time systems might be found in elevator controls, vending machines and gas pumps, smart washing machines, and such. Most real time systems have a mix of both hard and soft real time sections.

The software state machine is a valuable concept in embedded systems. A *state machine* does its transitions as a function of current state, and inputs. These can be implemented in software or hardware. They are useful in the areas of control-dominated code, and reactive systems. A real time systems changes state as a function of time, or events. A hard real time system is in synchronism whit its environment.

Some of the tools we can apply to our architecture and design will be discussed. In many cases, we can apply a data flow architecture, which has very simple control structures, but operates on a stream of data. We can build a simple data flow graph, showing inputs, operations, and outputs. On the other hand, we might have a heavily control-flow architecture, where there are asynchronous events, and numerous decision point and paths through the code. Here, we can also represent this in graph format, with 2 types of nodes, decision, with two or more outputs, and data flow. The control flow can capture such constructs as if-then-else, do-while, and for-do.

Scheduling of tasks can be done statically, or dynamically. Static scheduling is done at compile time. It's advantage is low run-time overhead. Dynamic scheduling is done at run time, and this involves overhead. Static and dynamic scheduling can be preemptive or non-preemptive. In the preemptive case, the currently running task is suspended when a higher priority task is ready to run. In the non-preemptive case, the currently running task is allowed to complete.

There are numerous algorithms for real-time scheduling, and we'll discuss a few of the more popular ones. In the rate monotonic case, There are static priorities, assigned by task period (the repeat time of the task. Rate monotonic is a dynamic scheduler. The algorithm in the scheduler assigns the highest priority to the task with the shortest period. At run time, the scheduler selects the task with the highest priority for execution.

RTOS

In a real-time system, the timing of the result is as important as the logical correctness. Embedded systems find themselves in these situations a lot. There are two types of deadlines, hard and soft, and various scheduling policies to address these. A scheduling policy should have the ability to meet all deadlines. The scheduling overhead should be minimal.

In soft real time, the average performance or response time is emphasized. Desktops and servers can meet soft real time requirements. Missing a deadline is not necessarily catastrophic. It may result in a degradation of service, but not a failure.

In hard real time, on the other hand, critical sections of code have absolute deadlines, regardless of how busy the system is. Missing a deadline means system failure. Response times must be deterministic. Examples of hard real time systems include most spacecraft avionics.

Interestingly, meeting a deadline early may be just as bad as meeting it late. There may be constraint requirements on the response time window for the systems, and too many resources consumed in being early that make other processes late.

We can have systems with the characteristics of both; these multi-rate systems handle operations and deadlines at varying rates.

Non-Real Time (NRT) systems are fair; they provide resources (time, I/O) to all users or programs on an equal, or pre-determined priority basis. They can arbitrate resource allocation to maximize the number of deadlines met, or minimize lateness, or some combination. Everyone gets a turn. NRT systems have high throughput and fast average response.

Multiple approaches to scheduling have evolved, and we'll discuss some of them here.

In Round Robin scheduling, we can bound maximum CPU load, but may leave unused CPU cycles. The scheduling can be adapted to handle an unexpected load. We want to use all the available time slots by the end of period. We will schedule tasks that are ready, and use equal time intervals. Of course, if a ready low priority task can lock out a not-yet-ready high priority task, we have a problem. This is not a good approach for hard real time.

Not all CPU time is available for processes, some is used for operating system overhead. The scheduling process itself consumes CPU time. Scheduling overhead must be taken into account for the exact schedule.

To evaluate and define the worst case, we need to examine the requirements, and the implementation design in terms of the cpu, the program that is running, the specific task that is addressing the worst case, the context of the operating system, and other software activities. We can ensure meeting deadlines by hardware or software, or both. We can develop faster or smarter software, or choose faster hardware.

One approach is the use of a cyclic executive. Here, a timer triggers a task every frame. This is a periodic interrupt. Timers are the on-chip peripherals that are used by the scheduler.

When using event driven programming, some events are asynchronous to the system, and the embedded system must react to them. We determine our latency requirements and program our system accordingly. However, many events need to be tightly synchronized to a specific clock.

Timers allow us to perform event-driven operations on an accurate time-scale without tying up our processor, providing deterministic performance. Timers give us greater time resolution than we could accomplish (easily at least) using sequential programming techniques.

We need to generate a predefined list of tasks that the systems will accomplish, based on the system requirements. If we need concurrency, we will require a synchronization mechanism. We are trying to achieve a predictive response under all conditions. We also need to know data dependencies between processes. We need to profile the software to define the execution times, average and worst case.

There are multiple *real time scheduling policies*, which are tailored to the application domain and its requirements. Each task has an associated priority. The resources are allocated to the highest priority task that is ready. Priorities determine the scheduling process. Priorities can be fixed or time-varying. The problem becomes whether the system can meet all required deadlines. One solution is to increase the cpu speed. You do this by waiting for the next generation of hardware. But, faster systems can also consume more power, and dissipate more heat.

We also may have *aperiodic processes*, which execute on demand, controlled by asynchronous external processes.

In the *Fixed Priority Preemptive scheme*, a higher priority task can preempt a lower priority task. In the *Rate Monotonic* scheme, the higher the frequency of a task, the higher its priority.

We always need to keep in mind the context switch overhead; there is a finite amount of time and resources required to switch tasks (or threads of execution). This is the task switch overhead.

Real-time tasks share resources for which they contend, and they may be forced to wait.

Priority inheritance protocols bound priority inversion. Real time operating systems generally use a priority based preemptive scheduler. Each task has a unique priority based on system requirements. Tasks have an associated state, running, ready, or waiting. A scheduler program ensures that of the list of ready tasks, the highest priority one is running. A lower priority task may be preempted. A problem may occur because of shared resources. In *priority inversion*, the highest priority task fails to run when it should due to a shared resource conflict.

Priority inversion was demonstrated on the surface of Mars in July 1977 during the Pathfinder Mission. A higher priority task was forced to wait for a lower priority task, due to shared resource contention. A lower priority task had control of a resource that it needed to access until completion. This locked out the critical higher resource task. It was successfully identified and fixed, remotely, from another planet.

In unbounded priority inversion, we have multiple medium priority tasks. The tasks are periodic. If we have a lower priority task holding a critical resource, and a medium priority tasks preempt the lower priority task, which can't complete, we have a problem. And, since the tasks are periodic, they keep getting rescheduled, and the problem continues.

In a priority inheritance protocol, a task runs at its original priority, unless it is blocking a higher priority task. Then, it runs at the priority of the higher level task it is blocking. Mutual deadlocks are possible; this is the deadly embrace scenario. Here, neither task can proceed until the other allows it.

In the *Priority ceiling* protocol, no task can be blocked for longer than the duration of the longest critical section of a lower priority task, instead of for the entire duration of the lower priority task. Aperiodic tasks are non-periodic events with no fixed deadlines, but they interfere with periodic tasks.

Soft Realtime

Operating Systems designed for the desktop were developed under the assumption that whatever resources are required will be available. They are also *fair* in the sense of allocating resources without priorities. These are fine for desktop applications and servers, even some soft real time systems. Both proprietary and Open Source operating systems are applicable for soft real time systems. Be careful in their use, because they bring a lot of functions along with them that are not applicable to the embedded world.

One open source solution is a clever Linux distribution called Linux from Scratch. This is a bottoms-up approach to generating a custom Linux distribution. For the desktop, you generally get a Linux with just about everything included, and add to it what you need. In the embedded world, you need a lean-and-mean operating system. With Linux from Scratch, you only include the modules you need. If your spacecraft has no video, you don't need to include video drivers in the package. There is a learning curve in building operating systems from modules, but it is an interesting approach to optimization.

Hard real time

Real-time operating systems, as opposed to those addressing desktop, tablet, and server applications, emphasize predictability and consistency over throughput and low latencies. Determinism is probably the most important feature in a real-time operating system.

A microkernel operating system is ideally suited to embedded systems. It is slimmed down to include only those features needed, with no additional code. Barebones is the term often used. The microkernel handles memory management, threads, and communication between processes. It has device drivers for only those devices present. The operating systems may have to be recompiled when new devices are added. A file system, if required, is run in user space. MINIX, as an example of a streamlined open-source kernel, and has about 6,000 lines of code.

Some example off-the-shelf RTOS include:

<u>VxWorks</u>

VxWorks is a commercial real-time embedded operating system and associated Integrated Design Environment from Wind River. It is widely used in the embedded world. VxWorks is not open source. It has a multitasking kernel with preemptive and round-robin scheduling and fast interrupt response. Symmetric multiprocessing is supported. Several file systems are also supported. A wide range of target architectures are available, both chip-level, and board level products. Wind River also has a version of Gnu-Linux, derived from RTLinux, called WindRiver Linux 5. Currently, VxWorks is the operating system of choice for Mars exploration rovers.

<u>Real Time and embedded Linux</u>

There are several approaches to make GNU/Linux a real-time operating system. One version developed by FSM labs, and used by VxWorks, is a hard real-time RTOS microkernel that runs the entire Gnu-Linux operating system as a fully preemptive process. To address soft real-time, the GNU/Linux kernel can be modified by several available patches to add non-preemption and low latency, with a deterministic scheduler.

The standard GNU/Linux (or BSD) kernel is not pre-emptable. This means kernel code runs to completion. The run time is not bounded, which interferes with responding to time-critical events. It is important to keep in mind that the Gnu-Linux kernel was not designed for non-preemption, as a true real-time operating system would be. Preemption has overhead, and influences throughput, usually adversely. There is a real-time Linux Foundation (.org) that is a good source of information on these topics.

<u>LynxOS</u>

The LynxOS RTOS is a Unix-like real-time operating system from

LynuxWorks It is a real-time POSIX operating system for embedded applications. LynxOS components are designed for absolute determinism (hard real-time performance), which means that they respond within a known period of time. Predictable response times are ensured even in the presence of heavy I/O due to the kernel's unique threading model, which allows interrupt routines to be extremely short and fast. LynuxWorks has a specialized version of LynxOS called LynxOS-178, especially for use in avionics applications that require certification to industry standards such as DO-178B. This is titled, *Software Considerations in Airborne Systems and Equipment Certification, and* is a guideline for safety-critical software used in airborne and spaceborne systems. Although just a guideline, it is a *de facto* standard for developing avionics software systems.

RTEMS

RTEMS is the Real-Time Executive for Multiprocessor Systems, designed for embedded use, and free and open source. It is POSIX compliant. The TCP/IP stack from FreeBSD is included. RTEMS does not provide memory management, but is single process, multithreaded. Numerous file systems are supported. RTEMS is available for the ARM, Atmel AVR, and a wide variety of other popular embedded cpu's and DSP's. An RTEMS system is currently in orbit around Mars.

FreeRTOS

FreeRTOS is an open source, real time operating system. It supports many different cpu's. It has a pre-emptive scheduler, and a very small software footprint, 6-12k, and can be contained in ROM.

QNX

QNX is a real-time operating system based on Unix. QNX Neutrino RTOS is SMP capable, and supports POSIX APIs. It is not open source.

The QNX microkernel contains only CPU scheduling, inter-process communication, interrupt redirection, and timers. Everything else runs as a user process, including a special process known as *proc* which performs process creation, and memory management by operating in conjunction with the microkernel. There are no device drivers in the kernel. The network stack is based on NetBSD code.

Ubuntu Mobile and Embedded are variations of the Ubuntu Linux distribution for Mobile Phones, and embedded applications in general.

A Minimalistic approach

Don't feel up to writing and configuring your own operating system? One may not be needed. The operating system functions can be included within the user code in the simplest case. A simple polling loop (DO WHILE 2>1) provides the ability to check states, and interrupt servicing will allow asynchronous events to be handled. This approach can be based on a state machine design, or involve multiple interacting state machines. For simple systems, this is a good approach. But the software doesn't scale to more complexity easily, and determinism can soon be compromised. At some point, the use of an operating system can simplify the overall job.

Interrupts provide a response to external events, but in many cases, a polling loop will suffice. Interrupts are generally required in hard real time systems. Interrupts allow for non-sequential running of the code.

Interrupts can be synchronous or asynchronous. Most external interrupts are asynchronous to the processor. Internal interrupts, sometimes called exceptions, are synchronous,. These include page faults and attempted division by zero.

How do we measure interrupt latency? It is difficult to determine, and can usually only be bounded. Since we don't know when an asynchronous interrupt will occur in an instruction cycle, we can't precisely determine the latency. This is because, in almost all cases, the current instruction will always finish executing before the interrupt is acknowledged. All the instructions may not take the same time to execute, and we have to factor in cache and pipeline effects.

If there is no opsys, the functions are done within the user code. Not all the opsys functions are implemented, but only those needed. This results in one monolithic program. A lot of IDE's attach "operating system" function code to our user program, and we are not always aware of this. Code for startup (bootloader) and interrupt vector initialization is usually included, as well as serial I/O support.

We can implement our real time program as a "While" loop for several processes. Here we encapsulate a set of all processes in a single function that implements the task set. We use a timer to control execution of this task. We have no control over timing of individual processes, just the main loop. Alternately, we could use multiple timers, each process having its own.

CFE, cFS

The Core Flight Executive, from the Flight Software Branch (Code 582) at NASA/GSFC, is an open source operating system framework. The executive is a set of mission independent re-usable software services and an operating environment. Within this architecture, various mission-specific applications can be hosted. The CFE focuses on the commonality of flight software. The Core Flight System (CFS) supplies libraries and applications. Much flight software legacy went into the concept of the CFE. It has gotten traction within the NASA community, and is in use on many flight projects, simulators, and test beds (FlatSats) at multiple NASA centers.

The CFE presents a layered architecture, starting with the bootstrap process, and including a real time operating system. At this level, a board support package is needed for the particular hardware in use. Many of these have been developed. At the OS abstraction level, a Platform support package is included. The CFE core comes next, with cFE libraries and specific mission libraries. Ap's habituate the 5th, or upper layer. The CFE strives to provide a platform and project independent run time environment.

The boot process involves software to get the system configured and going after power-on, and is contained in non-volatile memory. CFE has boot loaders for the RAD750 (from BAE), the Coldfire, and the Leon3 architecture. The real time operating systems can be any of a number of different open source or proprietary products, VxWorks and RTEMS for example. This layer provides interrupt handling, a scheduler, a file system, and interprocess communication.

The Platform Support Package is an abstraction layer that allows the CFE to run a particular RTOS on a particular hardware platform. There is a PSP for desktop pc's for the CFE. The CFE Core includes a set of re-usable, mission independent services. It presents a standardized application Program Interface (API) to the programmer. A software bus architecture is provided for messaging between applications.

The Event services at the core level provides an interface to send asynchronous messages, telemetry. The CFE also provides time services.

Aps include a Health and Safety Ap with a watchdog. A housekeeping AP for messages with the ground, data storage and file manager aps, a memory checker, a stored command processor, a scheduler, a checksummer, and a memory manager. Aps can be developed and added to the library with ease.

A recent NASA/GSFC Cubesat project uses a FPGA-based system-on-a-chip architecture with Linux and the CFE. CFE and its associated cFS are available as an architecture for Cubesats in general.

The CFE has been released into the World-Wide Open Source community, and has found many applications outside of NASA.

NASA's software Architecture Review Board reviewed the CFE in 2011. They found it a well thought-out product that definitely met a NASA need. It was also seen to have the potential of becoming a dominant flight software architectural framework. The technology was seen to be mature.

The cFS is the core flight software, a series of aps for generally useful tasks onboard the spacecraft. The cFS is a platform and project independent reusable software framework and set of reusable applications. This framework is used as the basis for the flight software for satellite data systems and instruments, but can be used on other embedded systems in general. More information on the cFS can be found at http://cfs.gsfc.nasa.gov

OSAL

The OS Abstraction Layer (OSAL) project is a small software library that isolates the embedded software from the real time operating system. The OSAL provides an Application Program Interface (API) to an abstract real time operating system. This provides a way to develop one set of embedded application code that is independent of the operating system being used. It is a form of middleware.

cFS aps

CFS aps are core Flight System (cFS) applications that are plug-in's to the Core Flight Executive (CFE) component. Some of these are discussed below.

CCSDS File Delivery (CF)

The CF application is used for transmitting and receiving files. To transfer files using CFDP, the CF application must communicate with a CFDP compliant peer. CF sends and receives file information and file-data in Protocol Data Units (PDUs) that are compliant with the CFDP standard protocol defined in the CCSDS 727.0-B-4 Blue Book. The PDUs are transferred to and from the CF application via CCSDS packets on the cFE's software bus middleware.

Limit check (LC)

The LC application monitors telemetry data points in a cFS system and compares the values against predefined threshold limits. When a threshold condition is encountered, an event message is issued and a Relative Time Sequence (RTS) command script may be initiated to respond/react to the threshold violation.

Checksum (CS)

The CS application is used for for ensuring the integrity of onboard memory. CS calculates Cyclic Redundancy Checks (CRCs) on the different memory regions and compares the CRC values with a baseline value calculated at system start up. CS has the ability to ensure the integrity of cFE applications, cFE tables, the cFE core, the onboard operating system (OS), onboard EEPROM, as well as, any memory regions ("Memory") specified by the users.

Stored Command (SC)

The SC application allows a system to be autonomously commanded 24 hours a day using sequences of commands that are loaded to SC. Each command has a time tag associated with it, permitting the command to be released for distribution at predetermined times. SC supports both Absolute Time tagged command Sequences (ATSs) as well as multiple Relative Time tagged command Sequences (RTSs).

Scheduler (SCH)

The SCH application provides a method of generating software bus messages at pre-determined timing intervals. This allows the system to operate in a Time Division Multiplexed (TDM) fashion with deterministic behavior. The TDM major frame is defined by the Major Time Synchronization Signal used by the cFE TIME Services (typically 1 Hz). The Minor Frame timing (number of slots executed within each Major Frame) is also configurable.

File Manager (FM)

The FM application provides onboard file system management services by processing ground commands for copying, moving, and renaming files, decompressing files, creating directories, deleting files and directories, providing file and directory informational telemetry messages, and providing open file and directory listings. The FM requires use of the cFS application library

Data Storage (DS

The DS application is used for storing software bus messages in files. These files are generally stored on a storage device such as a solid state recorder but they could be stored on any file system. Another cFS application such as CFDP (CF) must be used in order to transfer the files created by DS from their onboard storage location to where they will be viewed and processed. DS requires use of the cFS application library.

Memory Manager (MM)

The MM application is used for the loading and dumping system memory. MM provides an operator interface to the memory manipulation functions contained in the PSP (Platform Support Package) and OSAL (Operating System Abstraction Layer) components of the cFS. MM provides the ability to load and dump memory via command parameters, as well as, from files. Supports symbolic addressing. MM requires use of the cFS application library.

Housekeeping (HK)

The HK application is used for building and sending combined telemetry messages (from individual system applications) to the software bus for routing. Combining messages is performed in order to minimize downlink telemetry bandwidth. Combined messages are also useful for organizing certain types of data packets together. HK provides the capability to generate multiple combined packets so that data can be sent at different rates.

Memory Dwell (MD)

The MD application monitors memory addresses accessed by the CPU. This task is used for both debugging and monitoring unanticipated telemetry that had not been previously defined in the system prior to deployment. The MD application requires use of the cFS application library .

Software Bus Network (SBN)

The SBN application extends the cFE Software Bus (SB) publish/subscribe messaging service across partitions, processes, processors, and networks. The SBN is prototype code and requires a patch to the cFE Software Bus code.

This is now included in the software library.

<u>Health and Safety (HS)</u>

The HS application provides functionality for Application Monitoring, Event Monitoring, Hardware Watchdog Servicing, Execution Counter Reporting (optional), and CPU Aliveness Indication (via UART).

Being open source, you can write your own cFS aps for specific applications, or modify existing ones. However, you should submit them back to the owner (NASA-GSFC) for review and validation so they become a part of the official package, and available to others.

The cFS software does not handle all of the onboard tasks, particularly those that are mission unique.

Impacts of software

Keep in mind, executing software consumes energy and requires time. This can be observed and measured. Early in the design phase, we need to apply the *Design for Testability* approach. It is similar to the Design for Test approach in hardware, where test points are provided early.

It is critically important to document at development time. You won't have time later in the design process. The documentation can flow from requirements to specification to implementation and test. In fact, it is possible to write the documentation before the software code. It will need to be updated later to match reality, of course.

Another good practice is to define data structures first, then the processing. We all tend to focus on the algorithm first, but clever choices of data structures will simplify the algorithm. If shortcuts are required for speed or space, be sure to document your assumptions, and your violations.

Libraries of code to address specific functions; device drivers, and other software is generally available. It is always good to check whether the software function you need has already be done. It is worth a day of research, downloading, and testing to save time. However, readily available software doesn't always fit your specific problem. It is generally poorly documented, and it may contain malware.

Purchasing or downloading software from an established vendor provides some level of trustworthiness but doesn't guarantee success. Look for software modules and libraries that are supported. Software tools are also available in proprietary and open source versions.

Optimizing embedded systems code

We can optimize the code along various dimensions. It is relatively straightforward to optimize in a particular dimension, but one must be aware that a corresponding effect will be felt in other dimensions. It is important to get the code working first; to have it logically correct before attempting to optimize it. We can optimizing for time, memory space, energy usage, or along other dimensions..

Performance analysis

Before you can optimize, you need to measure the performance and characteristics of the system.

The system performance is a function of the different elements of the target system. This includes the cpu, the memory, including the cache, the bus, and the I/O devices, as well as the software.

Bandwidth is an important element of performance. The bandwidth of memory (including cache), the system bus, the I/O, and other elements is of importance. Different system components run at different clock rates, and may have different path widths. We can increase bandwidth by widening the data paths, or increasing the clock rates.

Parallelism is a technique to accelerate applications by doing more than one thing at a time. Some tasks are inherently serial, and cannot be improved by parallelism. Some are "embarrassingly parallel." Multicore techniques provide parallelism at the CPU level The DMA technique increases I/O performance when there is no bus contention.

For real-time systems, we need to have visibility of the real-time behavior of our system. This varies with the input data, since the code is taking different paths. This also effects the cache behavior, and interacts with the pipeline architecture.

There are different ways to measure program performance. First, keep in mind that if you add additional code to your program, you are measuring the performance of your code plus the new. It is an old adage - "Test what you fly, fly what you test." If you remove the instrumentation code, you are left with a package you haven't tested yet. Think of it this way – the instrumentation code changes the load image. Things move around in memory and cache. When we execute the instrumented code, the instruction pipeline contents are different, and this affects interrupt latency. Just leave it in. It doesn't weigh anything.

There's an amusing story along those lines. I worked on a program to capture the design of the NASA Standard Spacecraft Computer (NSSC-1), originally implemented in some 4000 discrete gates, in an FPGA. We got it working, but noticed there were some logic units that didn't seem to be doing anything. We managed to contact the long-retired test technician for the unit, and asked him the question. After he stopped laughing, he explained how he had implemented a heart-beat function, with a little light, that he could see across the room. They removed the light, but the rest made it to orbit.

We could employ a simulator. These generally operate many orders of magnitude slower than the real program on the real hardware, but can be useful when we can isolate small, troublesome pieces of code. We can also measure the performance of the real code on the real hardware, by modifying our code with some instrumentation code, and using the timers. REMEMBER, the instrumentation code moves things around in the cache, makes the pipeline contents different, and sometimes introduces strange behavior on its own. We can also use a logic analyzer, if we have enough visibility of events, on pins that can be sampled. Some FPGA architectures allows for a built-in logic analyzer core.

What we're interested in defining is the worst case execution time. This depends heavily on the software interaction with the hardware in terms of speculative execution, pipelining, instruction issuance, and caches. Keep in mind that task level interactions can cause best-case program behavior to result in worst -case system behavior. We are interested in system behavior.

Execution time of a module of code has two parts, that of the program path, and the individual instruction timings. In a pure RISC machine, all instructions take the same amount of time. There are no pure RISC machines. Execution times of instructions are not independent. It depends on the instruction sequences. This is due to pipeline and cache effects. Also, execution time can be data dependent.

One key requirement is defining the test data sets that define the desired inputs and outputs, and test all the possible cases. Hopefully, this will also drive out the best and worst cases.

We can choose to instrument the program and collect trace data. This modifies the program. The data sets generated are large. This approach works well in cache analysis.

Here's a quick story about the bad effects of instrumentation code. Guy that worked for me on a mobile robotics project was really good, but no one else could read his code. Think, 100,000 lines of undocumented Pascal. Our office was on the second floor of a building with no elevator, and our robot weighed several hundred pounds. He worked in my garage. Every day he came to my house, and I went to the office. I wanted him to wrap it up and get out of my garage.

One day when I got home and asked him how close he was to finished, it triggered a long stream of technical programming details about strange behaviors, ghost paths through the code, non-deterministic behavior and demonic possession. At the end of which I said, "Where's your stack?" Looked like I smacked him with a 2x4. He went back to furiously typing. In about an hour he had everything working perfectly. Turn out he stored instrumentation data on the stack, and frequently overflowed it, causing his data to be executed.

Other devices that help in debugging real-time are in-circuit emulators, which also effect execution timing, and logic analyzers, which can also see whats on the pins, not what's inside. These can be combined with simple mods to the program to output special patterns that can be scanned for. Again, we modify the code.

Optimizing for execution time

Optimizing a program for run time is a common technique. One of the more important aspects of the situation is to get the program logically correct first, and then analyze it for "hot spots." These can be optimized for time, and then regression-tested. A lot of techniques have been developed for this. Optimizing compilers are available, based on these principles. One popular technique is loop unrolling. With a loop, we have a certain number of operations, repeated "n" times, plus the overhead of the loop. If we unroll this into linear, yet repeated, code, we can save time, at the expense of additional program space.

Sometimes, we can replace a piece of higher level code with an assembly language module optimized for that particular function. We also need to consider the effects of data structures and their organization on run time. This is particularly true for vectors or arrays of data. How we arrange the data, compared to the physical layout of memory or cache can drastically effect access time. For example, if we have two arrays to multiply, and a cache size of 4 kilobytes, we better hope the arrays are not 4 kilobytes + 1 byte long. This will result in severe cache thrashing. Physical entities such as roll, path, yaw can be mapped into a convenient 4-unit vector by adding one dummy element, making them much more compatible to caching, which deals with powers-of-2 sizes.

Some common techniques involve faster mathematics. If we identify multiplication and division by constants, we can handle this without multiply and divide instructions. This usually takes the visibility we only get at the assembly language level. Assembly language programming is more complicated because the programmer is responsible for a lot of the detail that would be taken care of by the compiler. However, this means a corresponding increase in the level of control of the process. Assembly language results in one machine instruction per line of code, as opposed to a line of higher level language, which results in multiple lines of machine code.

Assembly language is unique to each processor type, as opposed to higher level languages such as c that are fairly consistent across different implementations. There is a larger set of details for the programmer to keep track of at the assembly language level. In higher order languages, these details are handled by the language compiler.

Optimizations are important to document, because the resultant code is usually not immediately obvious as to its function.

Another approach to performance is to wait for the next generation of chip, which should be out within the year. It will be faster, have more memory, have better I/O. Stall. Tell your boss you're "conducting trade studies."

In terms of performance optimization, we can hand-optimize the code, but keep in mind the cpu does not execute c or Java. We need to optimize the machine language. Compilers are very good at optimizing the HOL, although many of the optimizations will be non-obvious.

Optimizing for memory size

We might run into a situation where 1 more byte in program or data size will force us to add a second memory device, or need to add an external memory to a cpu chip with limited internal storage. Optimizing for size might be required. At the same time that memory gets larger and larger, riding the Moore's law curve, programs and data structures get more and more complex. More memory means more power dissipated. We can trade computation for size in some cases.

Optimizing for energy or power

We may also be interested in optimizing code for minimum power consumption or minimum energy usage. The ultimate approach is for the system to go to sleep or be suspended when possible, and be awakened by a periodic interrupt or upon demand. This assumes it can maintain state while asleep.

Optimization for power can be implemented in hardware, software, or a mix. Some hardware platforms support dynamic voltage or frequency scaling. The system may run at different clock frequencies at different time, ramping up to complete a critical algorithm, then slowing down again. Power consumption is proportional to the square of the voltage. As long as the circuitry can distinguish between the two logic states, we are good.

The Opsys can determine how system resources are scheduled/used to control power consumption. The OS can manage for power just as it manages for time. The OS reduces power by shutting down units. The cpu itself may have partial shutdown modes. Power management and performance are often at odds. Entering a power-down mode itself consumes energy and time. Leaving power-down mode also consumes energy and time.

How do we implement power efficient code? First, we have to have the proper instrumentation. It may be a simple matter to hook an ammeter between the power supply and the computer board. This gives us baseline profile values. Then, we need to identify the power consuming items. Some of these we can't change – those that are soldered on the board, without a redesign. The cpu may have a throttle-down mode to reduce power draw. Non-rotating memory does not use significantly more power in operation than in idle. Power reduction and monitoring in real time can be an operating system task. With proper instrumentation in the software and hardware, we can profile the watt-hours per algorithm. Test and development tool vendors such as Mentor Graphics provide power and energy analysis tools.

Energy consumption has a sweet spot as cache size changes. If the cache is too small: the program thrashes, burning energy on external memory accesses. If the cache is too large, the cache itself burns too much power. What is the right size? This can be determined by analysis, simulation, and testing.

Optimizing for energy consumption involves the efficient use of registers. We also need to identify and eliminate cache conflicts. In this area, moderate loop unrolling eliminates some loop overhead instructions. We also need to focus on eliminating pipeline stalls. In-lining procedures may help; this reduces linkage overhead, but may increase cache thrashing. Again, simulation helps to provide visibility into the process.

Besides the cpu and the memory, the I/O devices and interfaces consume power. Wireless devices use a fair amount of power, but can be power-cycled by the software to minimize their power profile. USB devices can be commanded to shut down or suspend operation. More advanced power management is integrated into the later chipsets and cpu's.

At the current writing, the benchmark of performance efficiency for ground-based products is around one gigaflop per watt. This is expected to improve an order of magnitude or two every few years.

Flash memory works better with sequential writes, and random reads. Flash can also be read indefinitely, but has a maximum number of times it can be written. It does "wear out." If we used flash as ram, or for a swap disk, we might exceed the write count in a matter of minutes or seconds. Writing to flash takes more power than having it sit idle. Flash is written to in blocks, and read in words. A block contains multiple words.

Smaller code may lead to power savings, because it uses less memory. Of course, memory comes in standard sizes, and we may not have the luxury of eliminating blocks of it. Putting code and data into low power cache, and power-cycling the main memory may be an applicable approach.

If we have the ability, we may power-cycle special purpose hardware such as the floating point units, the graphics or vector processor, and the analog/digital circuitry. We need to consider the start-up and settling time of the devices. We also might use frequency scaling, as the majority of energy is used to switch states.

Power consumption relates to heat generation. How hot is your software? It is too hot, you might need to include active cooling, which uses more power. In certain low-temperature environments, the "waste" heat from the processor might be useful in keeping circuitry and batteries from getting too cold. Real components don't like extremes of temperature, either too little or too much. Lower power systems need smaller power sources, which are smaller and lighter, and less expensive. Sometimes, you do get something for free. ACPI is a standard for power management services.

ITAR

Systems that provide "satellite control software" are included under the *International Trafficking in Arms* (ITAR) regulation, as the software is defined as "munitions" subject to export control. The Department of State interprets and enforces ITAR regulations. It applies to items that might go to non-US citizens, even citizens of friendly nations or NATO Partners. Even items received from Allies may not necessarily be provided back to them. Software and embedded systems related to launch vehicles and satellites are given particular scrutiny. The ITAR regulations date from the period of the Cold War with the Soviet Union. Increased enforcement of ITAR regulations recently have resulted in American market share in satellite technology declining. A license is required to export controlled technology. This includes passing technical information to a foreign national within the United States. Penalties of up to $100 million have been imposed for violations of the ITAR Regulations, and imprisonment is also possible. Something as simple as carrying ITAR information on a laptop or storage medium outside the US is considered a violation. ITAR regulations are complex, and need to be understood when working in areas of possible application. ITAR regulations apply to the hardware, software, and Intellectual Property assets, as well as test data and documentation. It is a complex topic.

Flight Software Complexity

There was a 2009 study of the Complexity of Flight Software with Headquarters and most of the Field Centers participating. The sponsor was the NASA Office of the Chief Engineer. There charter was to "Bring forward deployable technical and managerial strategies to effectively address risks from growth in size and complexity of flight software."

The first issue addressed was that of growth in flight software size. They had plotted mission software size in terms of lines of code pr year of mission, and gotten an exponential growth curve, with a 10x growth every 10 years, from 1968 to 2004. they had seen similar growth curves in Defense Systems, aircraft, and automobiles.

Software size, in terms of lines of code, is an indicator of complexity. Not a great indicator, but certainly one that can be measured.

Then, they set off to define complexity of software. This involves not only the number of components of a system, but also their inter-relationships. This leads to that fact that a systems has a certain essential complexity, which comes from the problem being addressed. There is also extraneous or incidental complexity, that gets added because of the solution chosen. Essential complexity comes from the problem domain and the requirements. The only way to reduce it is to downscope the problem. It can be moved later to operations, but not erased.

One of the major finding was that "Engineers and scientists often don't realize the downstream complexity entailed by their decisions." It was also noted that "...NPR 7123, NASA System Engineering Requirements, specifies in an appendix of "best typical practices" that requirements include rationale, but offers no guidance on how to write a good rationale or check it."

One good recommendation was that Software Architecture was a little-known or well understood element of software design, but an essential one. Another finding, in the NASA context, was that often a specific optimized design vastly increases operational complexity. Incidental complexity, though, comes from design choices.

They found that COTS software was a mixed blessing, in that it comes with features not needed. Although not needed, these features require additional testing, and increase the complexity. And, it is more complex to understand and remove them, then to test them.

One of the "take-away" messages was that flight software (read, embedded software) is increasing in complexity because we are solving increasing complex problems. One solution is to address complexity with architecture.

They quote a 1968 NATO report with the same concerns for the same reasons, although they considered 10,000 lines of code as complexity, then.

NASA recommended more emphasis on Fault Detection and containment.

They defined these characteristics for Flight Software:

"No direct user interfaces such as monitor and keyboard. All interactions are through uplink and downlink.

Interfaces with numerous flight hardware devices such as thrusters, reaction wheels, star trackers, motors, science instruments, temperature sensors, etc.

Executes on radiation-hardened processors and microcontrollers that are relatively slow and memory-limited. (Big source of incidental complexity)

Performs real-time processing. Must satisfy numerous timing constraints (timed commands, periodic deadlines, async event response). Being late = being wrong."

An interesting chart derived for JPL Missions (planetary) shows a vertical axis of software size times processor speed (bytes, mips) and a horizontal axis of time, where the curve through various missions is linear; ie, exponential growth, with a doubling time under two years.

The study pointed out that each step of the lifecycle process, requirements, design, coding and testing, both removed defects, and inserted new one. Thus, there are residual defects that ship with the system. Some of these are never found.

We can focus on reducing the defect insertion rate, or increasing the removal rate, but the bad news is, we'll never drive the rate to zero. Thus, there will be residual defects at launch. From empirical evidence, 1 million lines of code will have 900 benign defects, 90 medium level, and 9 potentially fatal. (Wait, did we say a card had 100 million lines of code?) This is based on a count of 1 residual defect per 1000 lines of code, an across-industries average for embedded code. What this leads us to conclude is that there is a current upper limit to system software complexity, measured in lines of code, because, beyond a certain size, the probability of mission failure tends to 1.

Architecture of a embedded or flight system is an essential part of the development process. Architecture tells us what we are building, not necessarily how. The architecture phase of system engineering has been slow to be adopted. The principles noted are that:

- "Architecture is an abstraction of a system that suppresses some details.
- Architecture is concerned with the public interfaces of elements and how they interact at runtime.
- Systems comprise more than one structure, e.g., runtime processes, synchronization relations, work breakdown, etc. No single structure is adequate.
- Every software system has an architecture, whether or not documented, hence the importance of architecture documentation.
- The externally visible behavior of each element is part of the architecture, but not the internal implementation details.
- The definition is indifferent as to whether the architecture is good or bad, hence the importance of architecture evaluation."

As things get more and more complex, even everyday things, we need to develop better ways to develop and verify software, whether it flys in space, or runs on our phone.

Whether we are working with systems, hardware, or software, we need to bound and control the complexity.

BIST

Built-in self-test is part of the design-for-testability philosophy. It is applicable at the box, board, or chip level. It defines the inclusion of additional circuitry or code specifically for testing purposes. It may include software components, or diagnostic cores for FPGA's. For example, when a standard pc system is reset, the initial code, in the BIOS, performs a series of functional tests on the hardware of the board hardware. This is generally referred to as POST – Power-On-Self-Test. The technique of BIST was first used operationally on the Minuteman missile.

EDAC

Memory scrubbing, where we read the memory locations and re-write them, is used in mitigation radiation of hits to memory. It is effectively a refresh operation, and can be implemented as a background, transparent refresh, using dram- refresh techniques, implemented in hardware or software.

Another approach involves only making critical parts rad-hard, for example, the newest SpaceCube's use the newer Virtex-5 architecture, which is available in a radiation hardened version. Previous versions used the commercial version, with a "Rad hard by Architecture" approach. The four integral processors provide a quad-redundant system, and a small, inherently radiation-hard processor serves as the voting device.

Standards

There are many Standards applicable to flight embedded systems. These range from general computer standards to embedded-specific, to flight-specific standards. Why should we be interested in standards? Standards represent an established approach, based on best practices. Standards are not created to stifle creativity or direct an implementation approach, but rather to capture the benefits of previous experience. Adherence to standards implies that different parts will work together. Standards are often developed by a single company, and then adopted by the relevant industry. Other standards are mandated by large customer organizations such as the Department of Defense, or the automobile industry. Many standards organizations exist to develop, review, and maintain standards.

Standards exist in many areas, including hardware, software, interfaces, protocols, testing, system safety, security, and certification. Standards can be open or closed (proprietary).

Hardware standards include the form factor and packaging of chips, the electrical interface, the bus interface, the power interface, and others. The JTAG standard specifies an interface for debugging.

In computer architecture, the ISA specifies the instruction set and the operations. It does not specify the implementation. Popular ISA's are x86 (Intel) and ARM (ARM Holdings, LTD). These are proprietary, and licensed by the Intellectual Property holder to chip manufacturers.

In software, an API (applications program interface) specifies the interface between a user program, and the operating system. To run properly, the program must adhere to the API.

There are numerous Quality standards, such as those from ISO, and Carnegie-Mellon's CMM (Capability Maturity Model). CMM defines five levels of organizational maturity in a company or institution, and is independently audited. Language standards also exist, such as those for the ANSI c and Java languages. Networking standards include TCP/IP for Ethernet, the CAN bus from Bosch, and IEEE-1553 for avionics.

The ISO-9000 standard was developed by the International Standards Organization, and applies to a broad range of industries. It concentrates on process. It's validation is based on extensive documentation of organization's process in a particular area, such as software development, system build, system integration, and test and certification.

It is always good to review what standards are available and could be applied to a space embedded system, as it ensures the application of best practices from experience, and interoperability with other systems.

The Portable Operating System Interface for Unix (POSIX) is an IEEE standard, IEEE 1003.1-1988. The standard spans some 17 documents. POSIX provides a Unix-like environment and API. Various operating systems are certified to POSIX compliance, including BSD, LynxOS, QNX, VxWorks, and others.

ARINC 653 is a software specification (API) for space and time partitioning in safety critical real-time operating systems. Each piece of application software has its own memory and dedicated time slot. The specification dates from 1996.

Flight systems electronics usually require MIL-STD-883b, Class-S, radiation-hard (total dose), SEU-tolerant parts. MIL-STD-883 is the standard for testing and screening of parts. Specific issues of radiation tolerance are discussed in MIL-M-38510. Class-S parts are specifically for space-flight use. Because of the need for qualifying the parts for space, the state-of-the-art in spaceborne electronics usually lags that of the terrestrial commercial parts by 5 years.

NASA's standard for parts selection, screening, qualification, and derating is NASA/TP-2003-212242.

Cubesats are defined by standards. A 1-U(nit) cubesat has a volume of exactly one liter (10 cm cube), and a mass of no more than 1.33 kilograms. It usually is built from COTS components. A Cubesat can also be built in a 3U, 6U, and 12U form factor. Part of the standardization of the structure ensures compatibility with the carrier and deployment system. The communications protocols are specified.

Structural materials must have the same coefficient of thermal expansion as the deployment mechanics to prevent jamming. Specifically allowed materials are four Aluminum alloys: 7075, 6061, 5005, and 5052. Aluminum used on the structure which contacts the P-POD must be anodized to prevent cold welding in vacuum. Other materials may be used for the structure with a proper waiver.

Technology Readiness Levels

The Technology readiness level (TRL) is a measure of a device's maturity for use. There are different TRL definitions by different agencies (NASA, DoD, ESA, FAA, DOE, etc). TRL are based on a scale from 1 to 9 with 9 being the most mature technology. The use of TRLs enables consistent, uniform, discussions of technical maturity across different types of technology. We will discuss the NASA one here, which was the original definition from the 1980's.

Technology readiness levels in the National Aeronautics and Space Administration (NASA)

Technology readiness level	Description

1. Basic principles observed and reported	This is the lowest "level" of technology maturation. At this level, scientific research begins to be translated into applied research and development.
2. Technology concept and/or application formulated	Once basic physical principles are observed, t hen at the next level of maturation, practical applications of those characteristics can be invented' or identified. At this level, the application is still speculative: there is not experimental proof or detailed analysis to support the conjecture.
3. Analytical and experimental critical function and/or characteristic proof of concept	At this step in the maturation process, active research and development (R&D) is initiated. This must include both analytical studies to set the technology into an appropriate context and laboratory-based studies to physically validate that the analytical predictions are correct. These studies and experiments should constitute "proof-of-concept" validation of the applications/ concepts formulated at TRL 2.
4. Component and/or breadboard validation in laboratory environment	Following successful "proof-of-concept" work, basic technological elements must be integrated to establish that the "pieces" will work together to achieve concept-enabling levels of performance for a component and/or breadboard. This validation must be devised to support the concept that was formulated earlier, and should also be consistent with the requirements of potential system applications. The validation is "low-fidelity" compared to the eventual system: it could be composed of ad hoc discrete components in a laboratory.
5. Component and/or breadboard validation in relevant environment	At this level, the fidelity of the component and/or breadboard being tested has to increase significantly . The basic technological elements must be integrated with reasonably realistic supporting elements so that the total applications (component-level, sub-system level, or system-level) can be tested in a 'simulated' or somewhat realistic environment.
6. System/subsystem	A major step in the level of fidelity of the

	technology demonstration follows the completion of TRL 5. At TRL 6, a representative model or prototype system or system - which would go well beyond ad hoc, 'patch-cord' or discrete component level breadboarding - would be tested in a relevant environment. At this level, if the only 'relevant environment' is the environment of space, then the model/prototype must be demonstrated in space.
model or prototype demonstration in a relevant environment (ground or space)	
7. System prototype demonstration in a space environment	TRL 7 is a significant step beyond TRL 6, requiring an actual system prototype demonstration in a space environment. The prototype should be near or at the scale of the planned operational s ystem and the demonstration must take place in space.
8. Actual system completed and 'flight qualified' through test and demonstration (ground or space)	In almost all cases, this level is the end of true 'system development' for most technology elements. This might include integration of new technology into an existing system.
9. Actual system 'flight proven' through successful mission operations	In almost all cases, the end of last 'bug fixing' aspects of true 'system development'. This might include integration of new technology into an existing system. This TRL does *not* include planned product improvement of ongoing or reusable systems.

TRL's can be applied to hardware or software, components, boxes, subsystems, or systems. Ultimately, we want the TRL level for the entire systems to be consistent with our flight requirements. Some components may have higher levels than needed.

The TRL assessment allows us to consider the readiness and risk of our technology elements, and of the system.

Flight Embedded Systems Security

Has your flight system been hacked? Are you sure?

All embedded systems have aspects of security. Some of these issues are addressed by existing protocols and standards for access and communications security. Security may also imply system stability and availability. Standard security measures such as security reviews and audits, threat analyses, target and threat assessments, countermeasures deployment, and extensive testing apply to the embedded domain.

A security assessment of a system involves threat analysis, target assessment, risk assessment, countermeasures assessment, and testing. This is above and beyond basic system functionality.

The completed functional system may need additional security features, such as intrusion detection, data encryption, and perhaps a self-destruct capability. Is that self-destruct capability secure, so not just anyone can activate it? All of these additional features use time, space, and other resources that are usually scarce in embedded systems.

Virus and malware attacks on desktops and servers are common, and an entire industry related to detection, prevention, and correction has been spawned. These issues are not as well addressed in the embedded world. Attacks on new technology such as cell phones, tablets, and GPS systems are emerging. Not all of the threats come from individuals. Some are large government-funded efforts or commercial entities seeking proprietary information or market position. Security breaches can be inspired by ideology, money, or fame considerations. The *CERT* (Computer Emergency Response Team) organization at Carnegie Mellon University, and the *SANS* Institute (SysAdmin, Audit, Networking, and Security) track security incidents.

Techniques such as hard checksums and embedded serial numbers are one approach to device protection. Access to the system needs to be controlled. If unused ports exist, the corresponding device drivers should be disabled, or not included. Mechanisms built into the cpu hardware can provide protection of system resources such as memory.

Security has to be designed in from the very beginning; it can't just be added on. Memorize this. There will be a quiz.

Even the most innocuous embedded platform can be used as a springboard to penetrate other systems. It is essential to consider security of all embedded systems, be aware of industry best practices and lessons learned, and use professional help in this specialized area.

The first detection of *backdoor code* in a military grade FPGA came in May of 2012. This was detected in an Actel ProASIC3 chip. It was built into the silicon and was activated by a secret key code. This caused much distress worldwide in the FPGA/ASIC world, and for their military customers. Although this was the first <u>detected</u> instance of this security breach, it was probably not the first instance. We can expect more of this type of behavior in the future of embedded systems anywhere.

Some example architectures

This section discusses selected example spacecraft embedded computer architectures.

NASA Standard Spacecraft Computer -1

The NSSC-1 was developed as a standard component for the Multi Mission Modular Spacecraft at GSFC in 1974. The basic spacecraft was built of standardized components and modules, for cost reduction. The computer had 18 bits of non-volatile core or plated wire memory; up to 64 k. 18 bits was chosen because it gave more accuracy (x4) for data over a 16 bit machine. Floating point was not supported.

The NSSC-1 was used on the Solar Maximum Mission (SMM), Space Telescope, and Landsat-D, among others. The hardware was developed by Westinghouse and NASA/GSFC. The machine used DTL (diode-transistor logic), the lowest power parts available at the time on the Preferred Parts List; Initially fabricated from 1700 SSI (nor-gate) packages, it was later updated to 69 MSI (medium scale integration) chips.

The NSSC-1 had an Assembler/loader/simulator toolset hosted on Xerox XDS 930 (24- bit) mainframe. An associated simulator ran at 1/1000 of real time. The Xerox computer was interfaced to a breadboard OBP in a rack, which operated at room temperature ambient conditions. Later, the Software Development and Validation Facility (SDVF) added a flight dynamics simulator hosted on a PDP-11/70 minicomputer.

A purpose-built NSSC-1 Flight Executive was developed and used on the SMM and subsequent flights. It time-sliced tasks at 25 ms. It included a stored command processor that handled both absolute time and relative time commands. It included a status buffer that could be telemetered back to the ground. It required a lot of memory, typically more than half of that available, leaving the rest for applications and spare.

The Space Telescope used a more advanced flight computer called the DF-

224 from Rockwell Autonetics for spacecraft control. The DF-224 was a 24-bit fixed point machine. It operated a 1.25 MHz, with 64 kilowords of memory. It was programmed in assembly language. There were three redundant CPU's, and 6 memory modules, using plated wire memory, a non-volatile technology similar to core. The computer weighed 110 pounds.

At the first servicing mission of the telescope by the Space Shuttle in 1993, a 16- MHz, dual redundant 80386/80387-based computer with 1 megabyte of ram designed at the Goddard Space Flight Center was added to the DF-224 to augment its capabilities. It interfaced by shared memory. The upgrade was possible because the DF-224 had accessible external electrical connectors. The upgrade by accomplished by astronaut extra-vehicular activity (EVA) operations.

The Third Servicing Mission in 2008 replaced the augmented DF-224 with a 50 MHz 80486-based computer that was radiation-hard.

References

NSSC-1 Onboard Flexibility for Space Missions, IBM Federal systems Division, Feb. 1978, 78-67K-001.

Trevathan, Charles E., Taylor, Thomas D., Hartenstein, Raymond G., Merwarth, Ann C., and Stewart, William N. "Development and Application of NASA's First Standard Spacecraft Computer," CACM V27 n9, Sept 1984, pp. 902-913.

Styles, F., Taylor, T., Tharpe, M. and Trevathan, C. "A General-Purpose On-Board Processor for Scientific Spacecraft," NASA/GSFC, X-562-67-202, July 1967.

Stakem, Patrick H. The History of Spacecraft Computers from the V-2 to the Space Station, 2009, PRB Publishing, ASIN B04L626U6..

Mars Science Laboratory Curiosity

The Mars Science Laboratory's lander, named *Curiosity*, landed successfully on the Martian surface on August 6, 2012. It had been launched on November

26, 2011. It's location on Mars is the Gale crater, and was a project of NASA's Jet Propulsion Laboratory. The project cost was around $2.5 billion. It is designed to operate for two Martian years (sols). The mission was to determine if Mars could have supported life.

The Rover vehicle weights just about 1 ton (2,000 lbs.) and is 10 feet long. It has autonomous navigation over the surface, and is expected to cover about 12 miles over the life of the mission. It uses six wheels

The Rover Compute Elements are based on the BAE Systems' RAD-750 cpu, rated at 400 mips. Each computer has 256k of EEprom, 256 Mbytes of DRAM, and 2 Gbytes of flash memory.

The power source for the rover is a radioisotope power system providing both electricity and heat. It is rated at 125 electrical watts, and 2,000 thermal watts, at the beginning of the mission.

The operating system is WindRiver's VxWorks real-time operating system.

ARM in Space

There have been numerous space projects utilizing the ARM processor. Among these, the Surrey Satellite Technology Nanosat Applications Platform (SNAP-1), which was launched on June 28, 2000. The onboard computer (OBC) was based on Intel's StrongARM SA-1100 with 4 Mbytes of 32-bit wide EDAC protected SRAM. The error correction logic corrected 2 bits in every 8 using a modified Hamming code and the errors are flushed from memory by software to prevent accumulation from multiple single-event upsets. There was 2 Mbytes of Flash memory containing a simple bootloader. The bootloader loaded the application software into SRAM. As will be discussed in the Cubesat section (below), the ARM-based Arduino and Raspberry Pi architectures are being used for Cubesat missions.

Suitsat

A PIC-18 microcontroller was used on NASA's SuitSat-1 in February 2006. SuitSat-1 was an actual Russian spacesuit, beyond its useful life, instrumented, inflated, and cast off from the International Space Station. The controller board used a Microchip PIC18F8722 8-bit microcontroller, MCP9800 temperature sensor, and MCP6022 op amps. Launch was easy – they just kicked it out the airlock,

1750A

The MIL-STD-1750 lays out a formal definition of a 16-bit instruction set architecture. It does not specify an implementation. The standard allows for memory mapping up to 2^{20} 16-bit words. There are 16 general purpose registers. Some can be used as index registers, some as base registers. Any register can be used as the stack pointer. Both 16 and 32-bit integer arithmetic are supported, as well as 32- and 48-bit floating point.

There are many implementations of the 1750A architecture, including several that are built as radiation-hardened pieces.

The preferred language for the 1750A was Jovial, an Algol language variant; later, ADA and c were used as well. The 1750A is found in many aircraft and missile applications by the United States Armed Forces and their allies. A quick list of examples include the USAF F-16 and −18, the AH-64D helicopter, and the F-111. The architecture is also used by the Indian Space Research Organisation (ISRO), and the Chinese Aerospace industry. In 1996, the 1750A architecture was declared obsolete for future military projects.

The 1750A found applications in many space projects, including NASA's Earth Observation Satellites (EOS) Aqua, Terra, and Aura. It was used on ESA missions Cluster and Rosetta. JPL used seven of the processors on the Cassini Mission to Saturn, and more units on Mars Observer and Mars Global Surveyor. It was used on the Clementine spacecraft, a NASA-Naval Research Laboratory Program to study the Moon. The 1750A was deployed on the Johns Hopkins University Applied Physics Laboratory's MSX − Midcourse Space Experiment spacecraft, which used nine. The 1750A flew on EUVE, MSTI -1, -2, & -3, Landsat-7, NEAR, and is on the GOES-13, GOES-O, and GOES−P NOAA spacecraft. The SPOT-4 mission includes a F9450, a National Semiconductor implementation. GEC-Plessy also manufactures a radiation-hard RH1750A.

Seven of the BAE-manufactured 1750A's went to Saturn on the Cassini Mission. These are part of BAE's Advanced Spaceborne Computer module (ASCM). BAE claims 200 of these modules are in orbit, in 2011.

Flight Beowulf

Beowulf refers to a parallel processing technique using multiple commodity pc's running linux, linked together. The technique has more recently been demonstrated by linking Raspberry Pi's. Flight Beowulf uses the technique for Cluster computing between members of a constellation of spacecraft.

Beowulf is a clustering technique developed at NASA's Goddard Space Flight Center based on commodity pc's as hardware, and the Parallel Virtual Machine (PVM) software, with the linux operating system. These heterogeneous inexpensive clusters provided a virtual supercomputer architecture. This technique came to be known as Grid computing. The Beowulf cluster meant that anyone could build a supercomputer.

PVM enabled the linking of inexpensive computation resources such as commodity pc's into supercomputing clusters. It was used by the University of Surrey to link several processing units on a satellite into a Beowulf cluster.

Cubesat

A Cubesat is a small, affordable satellite that can be developed and launched by college, high schools, and even individuals. The specifications were developed by Academia in 1999. The basic structure is a 10 centimeter cube, (volume of 1 liter) weighing less that 1.33 kilograms. This allows a series of these standardized packages to be launched as secondary payloads on other missions. A Cubesat dispenser has been developed, the Poly-PicoSat Orbital Deployer, that holds multiple Cubesats and dispenses them on orbit. They can also be launched from the Space Station, via a custom airlock. ESA, the United States, and Russia provide launch services. The Cubesat origin lies with Prof. Twiggs of Stanford University and was proposed as a vehicle to support hands-on university-level space education and opportunities for low-cost space access.

Cubesats can be custom made, but there has been a major industry evolved to supply components, including space computers. It allows for an off-the-shelf implementation, in addition to the custom build. There is quite a bit of synergy between the Amsat folks and Cubesats. NASA supports the Cubesat program, holding design contests providing a free launch to worthy projects. Cubesats are being developed around the world, and several hundred have been launched.

Build costs can be lower than $10,000, with launch costs ranging around $100,000, a most cost-effective price for achieving orbit. The low orbits of the Cubesats insure eventual reentry into the atmosphere, so they do not contribute to the orbital debris problem.

Central to the Cubesat concept is the standardization of the interface between the launch vehicle and the spacecraft, which allows developers to pool together for launch and so reduce costs and increase opportunities. As a university-led initiative, Cubesat developers have advocated many cost-saving mechanisms, namely:

- A reduction in project management and quality assurance roles
- Use of student labor with expert oversight to design, build and test key subsystems
- Reliance on non-space-rated Commercial-Off-The-Shelf (COTS) components
- Limited or no built-in redundancy (often compensated for by the parallel development of Cubesats)
- Access to launch opportunities through standardized launch interfaces
- Use of amateur communication frequency bands and support from amateur ground stations
- Simplicity in design, architecture and objective

The approach has since been adopted by numerous universities and organizations, and to date has been used as the basis of 40 missions (as at the end of October 2008) which have been launched since 2003, with many active projects in development. High schools and individuals are also pursuing Cubesat projects. The launch cost is a major issue, but multiple Cubesats can be carried as secondary payloads on military and commercial flights.

Since the initial proposal of the concept, further efforts have been made to define internal and external interfaces made by various developers of Cubesat subsystems, products and services that have defined the Cubesat 'standard' as it is today. A core strength of the Cubesat is its recognition of the need for flexibility in the definition of standards, and since conception the standard has evolved to ensure that these design rules are as open as possible. The most significant of these further advances in definition have been for the POD systems (in order to meet launch requirements) and the modularization of the internal electronics.

The in-orbit success rate of university-led Cubesat projects (not withstanding launch failures) is around 50%; this is an understandable result of using the

Cubesat as an education tool, where development itself is a learning process and in-orbit failure is a disappointment but should not be considered the primary focus. For projects involving significant participation of companies with experience in satellite development, all but one were a success and demonstrated the strength of the Cubesat for non-educational applications. It is estimated that at least 12 Cubesat missions could be considered to have demonstrated significant successful in-orbit operations for a sustained period. All Cubesats missions to date may be considered to have had technological objectives to some degree, be it the demonstration of devices and system architectures developed in-house, or demonstration of Non-Space-Rated (NSR) Commercial-Off-The-Shelf (COTS) component performance. Some Cubesats have also attempted to fulfill other mission objectives, although categorizing these accurately can be difficult

A simple Cubesat controller can be developed from a standard embedded platform such as the Arduino. The lack of radiation hardness can be balanced by the short on-orbit lifetime. The main drivers for a Cubesat flight computer are small size, small power consumption, wide functionality, and flexibility. In addition, a wide temperature range is desirable. The architecture should support a real time operating system, but, in the simplest case, a simple loop program with interrupt support can work.

Earth imaging is a common objective for a Cubesat mission, typically achieved using a CMOS camera without any complex lens systems. As a critical impediment to the development of a highly capable platform for mission operations, the testing and evaluation of novel approaches for increasing downlink data rate and reliability is also a common objective. While less common than Earth imaging, real science objectives are becoming increasingly popular as recognition (primarily by NASA) of Cubesat capabilities increase and collaborations between engineering and science groups emerge. Utility covers objectives not covered by the other categories and developed to handle a particular non-scientific demand.

Additional capabilities of proposed future missions either in planning or in development include: space weather monitoring, inflatable de-orbit devices, Earth imaging with optical lens, cosmic ray showers, shape memory alloys, star mapping, data relay, re-programmable computing, nano-meteorid dust, plasma probe, and multi-spectral remote sensing.

Cost reduction in these projects has been achieved through a number of mechanisms, some of which are unavailable to the conventional space industry. The lowest cost yet successful mission is reported to be estimated as under $100,000 (although the mission was not fitted with solar arrays). A typical cost for a university project varies considerably but a very approximate estimation might be from $50,000 to $150,000 for launch and $5-10,000. in parts cost per unit. Piggyback launches have been offered for free to Cubesats by launch vehicle operators and space agencies, negating the majority of launch cost.

Another important and related aspect in the design approach is that of modularity in a complete and integrated Cubesat life cycle, effectively representing a modular system of systems. The accelerated life cycle demonstrated consistently by small satellites, and harnessed by many Cubesat developers, can be further enhanced by the application of modularity to the complete life cycle. Cubesats are ideal teaching tools for aerospace engineering students , even if they are not going to fly.

Cubesat on - board computers

A simple Cubesat controller can be developed from a standard embedded platform such as the Arduino. The lack of radiation hardness can be balanced by the short on-orbit lifetime. The main drivers for a Cubesat flight computer are small size, small power consumption, wide functionality, and flexibility. In addition, a wide temperature range is desirable. The architecture should support a real time operating system, but, in the simplest case, a simple loop program with interrupt support can work. Both the Arduino and the Raspberry Pi, mentioned here, are based on the ARM architecture.

Arduino

The 32-bit implementation of the Arduino architecture is a strong candidate for Cubesat onboard computers. Many implementations feature a real-time clock, which is an add-on item in the Raspberry Pi architecture. A real time clock allows for the implementation of a real-time operating system. Cubesats with Arduinos have flown in orbit. The Arduino mini on the unit from Interorbital systems incorporates a current sensor to indicate a single event upset may have occurred due to radiation. The Arduino architecture has a relatively low tolerance to radiation damage (see, references, Violette).

The Raspberry Pi

The Raspberry Pi is a small, inexpensive, single board computer based on the ARM architecture. It is targeted to the academic market. It uses the Broadcom BCM2835 system-on-a-chip, which has a 700 MHz ARM processor, a video GPU, and currently 512 M of RAM. It uses an SD card for storage. The Raspberry Pi runs the GNU/linux and FreeBSD operating systems. It was first sold in February 2012. Sales reached ½ million units by the Fall. Due to the open source nature of the software, Raspberry Pi applications and drivers can be downloaded from various sites. It requires a single power supply, and dissipates less than 5 watts. It has USB ports, and an Ethernet controller. It does not have a real-time clock, but one can easily be added. It outputs video in HDMI resolution, and supports audio output. I/O includes 8 general purpose I/O lines, UART, I2C bus, and SPI bus.

The Raspberry Pi design belongs to the Raspberry Pi Foundation in the UK, which was formed to promote the study of Computer Science. The Raspberry Pi is seen as the successor to the original BBC Microcomputer by Acorn, which resulted in the ARM processor. The unit has enough resources to host an operating system such as linux.

Although the Raspberry Pi is not designed to be Rad hard, it showed a surprisingly good radiation tolerance in tests (in references, see Violette). It continued to operate through a dose of 150 krad(Si), with only the loss of USB connectivity.

If you want guaranteed performance with radiation hardened hardware, it will cost more, but quite a few vendors are available. Here are a few examples.

The NanoMind A712D is an onboard computer for Cubesats. It uses as 32-bit ARM cpu, with 2 megabytes of RAM, and 8 megabytes of flash memory. It can also support a MicroSD flash card. It has a Can bus and a I^2C interface. It comes with an extensive software library and real time operating system. Special applications, such as attitude determination and control code are available. It is tolerant to temperatures form -40 to 85 degrees C, but is not completely rad-hard.

The CFC-300 from InnoFlight Inc. of San Diego is another example. It uses the Xilinx Zynq System-on-a-chip architecture. That provides both FPGA capability, and an Arm Cortex A-9 dual core cpu. It has 256 Megabytes of SDRAM, and 32 megabytes of flash. There are multiple synchronous serial interfaces. Daughter cards provide support for SpaceWire, Ethernet, RapidIO,

RS-422, and thermistor inputs and heater drive outputs. It can be used with linux or VxWorks.

The Intrepid Cubesat OBC from Tyvak Uses a 400 MHz Atmel processor, and has 128 Mbytes of SDRAM, and 512 Mbytes of flash memory. It draws between 200-300 milliwatts. It includes a command and data handling system, and an onboard electrical power controller. It supports Ethernet, RS-232, USB, and the SPI and I^2C interfaces. It includes a JTAG debugging interface. Similar to the Arduino, it supports 3-axis gyros, a 3-axis magnetometer, accelerometers, and a variety of i^2c-interfaced sensors. The Microcontroller is an ARM architecture, with digital signal processing extensions. It has a built-in Image Sensor interface.

COVE is JPL's Xilinx Virtex-5 FPGA-based onboard processor for Cubesats. The FPGA is rad-hard. This high end machine provides sufficient power for onboard data processing, while providing a low power mode for periods where the number crunching is not needed. The FPGA can be reconfigured in flight. It has flown in space several times.

The Yaliny flight computer is based on the Microsemi Igloo-2 FPGA SOC. It is inherently SEU-immune. There is a soft processor core, implemented withing the FPGA. It has 8 megs of non-volatile, error-correcting memory, and 16 megs of static ram with error-correction. There is the ability to support 1 gigabyte of DDR SDRAM with error correction. It supports the 1553 bus, Ethernet, RS-485 quad pci-express busses, and usb (for debugging). The processor dissipates 2 watts nominally.

The proliferation of low cost and hobbyist grade Flight Computers can only have a positive effect on making the next generation of spacecraft smarter and cheaper.

At NASA and many National Labs, Cubesats have been a game-changer. The cost to develop, build, and test a concept or technology has gone down by orders of magnitude. This precursor technology has not only gone down in price, but the implementation process has been accelerated..

A recent NASA/GSFC Cubesat project, Dellingr, is set for launch as this book is being prepared. This will be a 6U (12" x 8" x 4") size. It was a one-year project to design, develop, test, and integrate the unit. It will be heading to the International Space Station. It is a Heliophysics payload, carrying an ion/neutral mass spectrometer. The design will be made available as Open Source after the mission is kicked off.

Another project was the NSF-funded Firefly mission, launched in November of 2013, and now returning good data on terrestrial Gamma ray flashes, These are interesting phenomena, involving high energy electrons generated by thunderstorms. Firefly uses a Pumpkin flight Motherboard for avionics, based on the Texas Instruments MSP430 chip. That unit is a 16-bit risc microcontroller architecture, The unit is ultra-low power, and mixed signal, supporting analog. It includes a real-time clock, and non-volatile FRAM memory.

Spacecube

The Space Cube Processor represents a family of reconfigurable architectures, using Xilinx Virtex-4 FPGA's with four integral PowerPC 405 450 MHz microprocessor cores. the SpaceCube was developed at NASA's Goddard Space Flight Center. The first SpaceCube into space was on the Hubble Servicing Mission 4, part of the Relative Navigation Sensors autonomous docking experiment. A subsequent mission (STS-129) carried a SpaceCube that was attached to the outside of the International Space Station, on the Naval Research Laboratory's MISSE7 experiment. SpaceCube is so-called because the packaging is a 4-inch cube. It uses less than 10 watts, and weighs less than four pounds. A unique stacking architecture is used for the mechanical and electrical inter-connection of the boards.

The follow-on SpaceCube's use the newer Virtex-5 architecture, which is available in a radiation hardened version. Previous versions used the commercial version, with a "Rad hard by Architecture: approach. the four integral processors provide a quad-redundant system, and a small, inherently radiation-hard processor serves as the voting device.

The FPGA in the SpaceCube has four instantiated PowerPC cpus, and the ability to instantiate more in the "sea of logic" that makes up the bulk of the device. The Xilinx "Microblaze" architecture is popular, and the chip can easily hold 16 of these devices, with an associated interconnect mechanism. The device can be reprogrammed or reconfigured in orbit.

The Xilinx FPGA's in non-radiation hardened versions, have flown on a variety of space missions, including the Australian FEDSAT mission, the Spirit and Opportunity Rovers on Mars, the MARS 2003 Lander and Rover, the Mars Science Laboratory, the Venus Express, TacSat-2, and others. Mitigation techniques for radiation effects include combinations of Triple Modular Redundancy (TMR), Error Detection and Correction (EDAC) circuitry, and memory scrubbing.

Test Environment

The engineering model of the spacecraft data system is generally referred to as the "FlatSat." It is used for integration and test. Early in the program, the Flatsat would consist of non-flight hardware. It is organized to fit on a table, with easy access to connections, functional boxes, and test points. As the project progresses, the data system will be built up of flight-like or flight boxes, and more care must be given to handling. Internal test points may not be easily accessed at this point in the program.

There is a major advantage to testing the flight system using software that will evolve into the operational environment. Previously, special test software was used, with scripting languages that facilitated testing. These are generally know as STOL – System Test Oriented Language.

Embedded Computer Systems in Space

This section will present a series of case studies, related to space embedded systems Some of these missions were resounding successes, and some resulted in failure.

Ariane 5 Launch Vehicle

Ariane 5's first test flight (Ariane 5 Flight 501) on 4 June 1996 failed, with the rocket self-destructing 37 seconds after launch because of a malfunction in the control software. A data conversion from 64-bit floating point value to 16-bit signed integer value to be stored in a variable representing horizontal bias caused a processor trap (operand error) because the floating point value was too large to be represented by a 16-bit signed integer. The software was originally written for the Ariane 4 where efficiency considerations (the computer running the software had an 80% maximum workload requirement) led to 4 variables being protected with a handler while 3 others, including the horizontal bias variable, were left unprotected because it was thought that they were "physically limited or that there was a large margin of error". The software, written in Ada, was included in the Ariane 5 through the reuse of an entire Ariane 4 subsystem despite the fact that the particular software containing the bug, which was just a part of the subsystem, was not required by the Ariane 5 because it has a different preparation sequence than the Ariane 4. The incident resulted in a loss of over $500 million.

Architecture, CPU, Memory, I/O

Thales Avionics

Software

Programmed in ADA; essentially the same as Ariane 4.

Sensors, Actuators

Input: Inertial reference system (IRS); output: nozzle vector control, via servo actuators

101

Root Cause

Flight control system failure. A diagnostic code from failed IRS-2 was interpreted as data. IRS-1 had failed earlier. The diagnostic data was sent because of a software error. The software module was only supposed to be used for alignment, not during flight. The diagnostic code was considered a 64-bit floating point number, and converted to a 16-bit signed integer, but the value was too large. This caused the rocket nozzles to steer hard-over to the side, causing the vehicle to veer and crash into a Mangrove swamp.

References

De Dalmau, J. and Gigou J. "Ariane-5: Learning from flight 501 and Preparing for 502, http://esapub.esrin.esa.it/billetin/bullet89/dalma89.html

Lions, Prof, J. L. (Chairman) ARIANE 5 flight 501 Failure, Report by the Inquiry Board, 19 July 1996, http://www.esrin.esa.it/tidc/htdocs/Press/Press96/ariane5rep.html

Jezequel, Jean-marc and Meyer, Bertrand "Design by Contract: The Lessons of Ariane," IEEE computer, Jan. 1997, vol. 30, n. 2, pp129-130.

"Inquiry Board Traces Ariane 5 Failure to Overflow Error," http://siam.org/siamnews/general/ariance.html

Baber, Robert L. "The Ariane 5 explosion as seen by a software engineer," http://www.cs.wits.ac.za/~bob/ariane5.htm.

Lunar Exploration

The latest mission to study the Moon is the Lunar Reconnaissance Orbiter, LRO, from NASA/GSFC. It was launched in 2009, and is still operating. It is is a polar orbit, coming as close as 19 miles to the lunar surface. It is collecting the data to construct a highly detailed 3-D map of the surface. Up to 450 Gigabits of data per day are returned to Goddard.

The LRO uses the RAD750 processor, on a CompactPCI 6U circuit card. The card provides a 1553 bus interface, and a 4-port Spacewire router. The cpu has 36 Megabytes of rad-hard sram, 4 megabytes of EEProm, and a 64k

ROM. The SpaceWire functionality is provided by an ASIC chip, with access to its own 8 megabytes of SRAM. The transport layer of the Spacewire protocol is implemented in the ASIC in hardware. The 1553 interface is implemented in an FPGA

The cpu operates with a 132 MHz clock, and the backplane bus runs at 66 MHz. It consumes between 5 and 19 watts of power, and weighs around 3.5 pounds.

The cpu communicates to other spacecraft electronics over the backplane cPCI bus, the 1553, or the Spacewire. The High data volume camera uses the SpaceWire interface at up to 280 MHz, and other instruments use the 1553. The onboard data storage for data is a 400 gigabit mass memory unit, using SDRAM.

Looking at the Sun

The Solar Terrestial Relations Observatory (Stereo) is a dual spacecraft mission to the Sun, launched in 2006. One is ahead of the Earth in orbit, the other behind. This gives three points of view of solar phenomena. Stereo's onboard computer uses the dual redundant Integrated Electronics Module (IEM) which has a RAD6000 cpu, as well as Actel FPGA's with soft-core P24 and CPU24 architectures. The P24 architecture is a 24-bit minimal instruction set computer (misc).

Venus Probes

The Soviet space program sent a series of probes to Venus. Early efforts were either crushed in the dense atmosphere, or suffered thermal damage. The Venera-7 mission had a goal of surface sample return. It struck the surface harder than planned, but returned temperature data for about 20 minutes. The Venera-8 probe returned data for some 50 minutes. Venera-13 and -14 returned color photos of the surface. Further Soviet efforts, and US efforts, involved observation from Venus orbit. The Venus environment has proven extremely hostile. It seems our sister world, next towards the Sun from us, is in a environmental runaway condition. Heavy greenhouse clouds trap the solar energy, and cause massive global warming on a planetary scale. The surface temperature is high enough to melt some metals. The only place this can be found on Earth is inside active volcanoes.

Mercury

The U. S. Messenger mission to Mercury, the closest planet to the Sun, was launched in 2004. It is currently orbiting the hottest planet. It's Integrated Electronics Module has two Rad-Hard RAD6000 processors. One is the main, the other is a fault protection processor, operating at a slower clock rate (10 MHz vs 25 MHz). The modules are also duplicated. Two solid stage data recorders with 1 gigabyte of storage capacity each are used

Mars Exploration

Mars Climate Orbiter

The spacecraft was lost on Mars in September 1999. The system-level requirements did not specify units, so JPL used SI units and the contractor Lockheed Martin used English units. This was not caught in the review process, and led to the loss of the $125 million mission. The spacecraft crashed due to a resulting navigation error.

Architecture, CPU, Memory, I/O

Single RAD6000 cpu, 128 megabytes ram, 18 megabytes flash.

Software

VxWorks operating system with flight software developed at Lockheed Martin Corp.

Sensors, Actuators

Dual 3-axis gyros, star tracker, dual sun sensors, 8 thrusters, 4 reaction wheels.

Root Cause

The primary cause of this discrepancy was human error. Specifically, the flight system software on the Mars Climate Orbiter was written to calculate thruster performance using the metric unit Newtons (N), while the ground crew was entering course correction and thruster data using the Imperial measure Pound-force (lbf). This error has since been known as the *metric mixup* and has been carefully avoided in all missions since by NASA.

"The root cause of the loss of the spacecraft was the failed translation of English units into metric units in a segment of ground-based, navigation-related mission software, as NASA has previously announced," said Arthur Stephenson, chairman of the Mars Climate Orbiter Mission Failure Investigation Board. "The failure review board has identified other significant factors that allowed this error to be born, and then let it linger and propagate to the point where it resulted in a major error in our understanding of the spacecraft's path as it approached Mars."

Reference

http://mars.jpl.nasa.gov/msp98/orbiter/

Mars Rover Pathfinder

The Mars Pathfinder mission landed on Mars on July 4, 1997. It carried a Rover named Sojourner, which was a 6-wheeled design, with a solar panel for power, but the batteries were not rechargeable. The rest of the lander served as a base station. Communication with the rover was lost in September. The Rover used a single Intel 80C85 8-bit CPU with a 2 MHz clock, 64k of ram, 16 k of PROM, 176k of non-volatile storage, and 512 kbytes of temporary data storage. It communicated with Earth via the base station using a 9600 baud UHF radio modem. The communication loss leading to end of mission was in the base station communication, while the Rover remained functional. The Rover had three cameras, and an x-ray spectrometer.

The computer in the mission base station on Mars was a single RS-6000 CPU, with 1553 and VMEbuses. The software was the VxWorks operating system, with application code in the c language. The base station computer experienced a series of resets on the Martian surface, which lead to an interesting remote debugging scenario.

The operating system implemented pre-emptive priority thread (of execution) scheduling. The watchdog timer caught the failure of a task to run to completion, and caused the reset. This was a sequence of tasks not exercised during testing. The problem was debugged from Earth, and a correction uploaded.

The cause was identified as a failure of one task to complete its execution before the other task started. The reaction to this was to reset the computer. This reset reinitialized all of the hardware and software. It also terminates the execution of the current ground commanded activities.

The failure turned out to be a case of priority inversion (how this was discovered and corrected remotely is a fascinating story – see refs.) The higher priority task was blocked by a much lower priority task that was holding a shared resource. The lower priority task had acquired this resource and then been preempted by several medium priority tasks. When the higher priority task was activated, it detected that the lower priority task had not completed its execution. The resource that caused this problem was a mutual exclusion semaphore used to control access to the list of file descriptors that the select() mechanism was to wait on.

The Select mechanism creates a mutex (mutual exclusion mechanism) to protect the "wait list" of file descriptors for certain devices. The vxWorks pipe() mechanism is such a device and the Interprocess Communications Mechanism (IPC) used was based on using pipes. The lower priority task had called Select, which called other tasks that were in the process of setting the mutex semaphore. The lower priority task was preempted and the operation was never completed. Several medium priority tasks ran until the higher priority task was activated. The low priority task attempted to send the newest high priority data via the IPC mechanism which called a write routine. The write routine blocked, taking control of the mutex semaphore. More of the medium priority tasks ran, still not allowing the high priority task to run, until the low priority task was awakened. At that point, the scheduling task determined that the low priority task had not completed its cycle (a hard deadline in the system) and declared the error that initiated the reset. The reset had the effect of wiping out most of the data that could show what was going on. This behavior was not seen during testing. It was successfully debugged and corrected remotely by the JPL team.

Architecture, CPU, Memory, I/O

Single RS-6000 cpu, 1553- and VMEbus.

106

Software

VxWorks, with application code in c.

Sensors, Actuators

Sun sensors, star tracker, radar altimeter, accelerometers, wheel drive.

Root Cause

Priority inversion in the operating system. Pre-emptive priority thread scheduling was used. The watchdog timer caught the failure of a task to run to completion, and caused the reset. This was a sequence of tasks not exercised during testing. The problem was debugged from Earth, and a software correction uploaded.

The failure was identified by the spacecraft as a failure of one task to complete its execution before the other task started. The reaction to this by the spacecraft was to reset the computer. This reset reinitializes all of the hardware and software. It also terminates the execution of the current ground commanded activities.

The failure was a classic case of priority inversion (The details of how this was discovered and corrected is a fascinating story – see refs.) The higher priority task was blocked by the much lower priority task that was holding a shared resource. The lower priority task had acquired this resource and then been preempted by several of the medium priority tasks. When the higher priority task was activated, to setup the transactions for the next 1553 bus cycle, it detected that the lower priority task had not completed its execution. The resource that caused this problem was a mutual exclusion semaphore used to control access to the list of file descriptors that the select() mechanism was to wait on.

The select mechanism created a mutual exclusion semaphore to protect the "wait list" of file descriptors for those devices which support select. The VxWorks pipe() mechanism is such a device and the IPC mechanism used is based on pipes. The lower priority task had called select, which had called other tasks, which were in the process of giving the mutex semaphore. The lower priority task was preempted and the operation was not completed. Several medium priority tasks ran until the higher priority task was activated. The low priority task attempted to send the newest high priority data via the IPC mechanism which called a write routine. The write routine blocked, taking the mutex semaphore. More of the medium priority tasks ran, still not allowing the high priority task to run, until the low priority task was awakened. At that point, the scheduling task determined that the low priority task had not completed its cycle (a hard deadline in the system) and declared the error that initiated the reset.

References

http://www.nasa.gov/mission_pages/mars-pathfinder/

http://research.microsoft.com/en-us/um/people/mbj/Mars_Pathfinder/

MER – Mars Exploration Rovers Spirit & Opportunity

The MER are six-wheeled, 400 pound solar-powered robots, launched in 2003 as part of NASA's ongoing Mars Exploration Program. *Opportunity* (MER-B) landed successfully at Meridiani Planum on Mars on January 25, 2004, three weeks after its twin *Spirit* (MER-A) had landed on the other side of the planet. Both used parachutes, a retro-rocket, and a large airbag to land successfully, after transitioning the thin atmosphere of Mars.

For power, they use 140 watt solar arrays and Li-ion batteries. The Rovers require 100 watts for driving, One problem that was noted was that the Martian dust storms cover the solar panels with fine dust, reducing their efficiency. This resulted in the use of a radioisotope generator on a subsequent mission. It's been observed that Rovers often use more energy in path planning, than to execute the actual path.

The onboard computer uses a 20 MHz RAD6000 CPU with 128 MB of DRAM, 3 MB of EEPROM, and 256 MB of flash memory on a VME bus. There is a 3-axis inertial measurement unit, and nine cameras The Rovers communicate with Earth via a relay satellite in Mars orbit, the Mars Global Surveyor spacecraft. They also have the ability to communicate directly, at a lower data rate.

The Spirit unit became stuck in 2009, and engineers were unable to free it after 9 months of trying. It was re-tasked as a stationary sensor platform. Contact was lost in 2010. Martian dust storms are very hard on solar panels.

This is an ongoing mission. It was originally planned for 90 days, but the *Opportunity* Rover is still collecting useful data regarding potential life on our sister planet some 11 years later as of this writing. It has traveled over 35 kilometers on the Martian surface. Ground based test units are used at JPL for evaluating problems seen on Mars, and for evaluating software and procedural fixes.

Mars Science Laboratory Curiosity

The Mars Science Laboratory's lander, named *Curiosity*, landed successfully on the Martian surface on August 6, 2012. It had been launched on November 26, 2011. It's location on Mars is the Gale crater, and was a project of NASA's Jet Propulsion Laboratory. The project cost was around $2.5 billion. It is designed to operate for two Martian years (sols). The mission is primarily to determine if Mars could have supported life in the past, which is linked to the presence of liquid water.

The Rover vehicle weights just about 1 ton (2,000 lbs.) and is 10 feet long. It has autonomous navigation over the surface, and is expected to cover about 12 miles over the life of the mission. The platform uses six wheels The Rover Compute Elements are based on the BAE Systems' RAD-750 CPU, rated at 400 mips. Each computer has 256k of EEprom, 256 Mbytes of DRAM, and 2 Gbytes of flash memory. The power source for the rover is a radioisotope thermal power system providing both electricity and heat. It is rated at 125 electrical watts, and 2,000 thermal watts, at the beginning of the mission. The operating system is WindRiver's VxWorks real-time operating system.

The computers interface with an inertial measurement unit (IMU) to provide navigation updates. The computers also monitor and control the system temperature. All of the instrument control, camera systems, and driving operations are under control of the onboard computers.

Communication with Earth uses a direct X-band link, and a UHF link to a relay spacecraft in Mars orbit. At landing, the one-way communications time to Earth was 13 minutes, 46 seconds. This varies considerably, with the relative positions of Earth and Mars in their orbits around the Sun,. At certain times, when they are on opposite sides of the Sun, communication is impossible.

The science payload includes a series of cameras, including one on a robotic arm, a laser-induced laser spectroscopy instrument, an X-ray spectrometer, and x-ray diffraction/fluorescence instrument, a mass spectrometer, a gas chromotograph, and a laser spectrometer. In addition, the rover hosts a weather station, and radiation detectors. There is cooperation between in-space assets and ground rovers in sighting dust storms by the meterological satellite in Mars orbit.

Maven

NASA's Maven mission to Mars is an orbiter studying the Martian atmosphere It was launched in November of 2013, and reached Mars in September of 2014.

MAVEN is equipped with a RAD-750 Central Processing Board manufactured by BAE Systems in Manassas, Va. The RAD750 CPU itself can tolerate 200,000 to 1,000,000 rads. Also, RAD750 will not suffer more than one radiation induced event requiring interventions from Earth over a 15-year period.

The RAD-750 was released in 2001 and made its first launch in 2005 aboard the Deep Impact Spacecraft. The CPU has 10.4 million transistors. The RAD750 processors operate at up to 200 megahertz, processing at 400 MIPS. The CPU has an L1 cache memory of 2 x 32KB (instruction + data) - to improve performance, multiple 1MB L2 cache modules can be implemented depending on mission requirements.

NEAR spacecraft

The Near Earth Asteroid Rendezvous – Shoemaker was launched in 1996 to study the asteroid Eros. It was a JHU/APL spacecraft, and a NASA mission. On Monday, 12 February 2001, the NEAR spacecraft touched down on asteroid Eros, after transmitting 69 close-up images of the surface during its final descent.

However, previously, the first of four scheduled rendezvous burns had been attempted on December 20, 1998. The burn sequence was initiated but immediately aborted. The spacecraft subsequently entered safe mode and began tumbling. The spacecraft's thrusters fired thousands of times during the anomaly, which expended 29 kg of propellant reducing the spacecraft's propellant margin to zero. This anomaly almost resulted in the loss of the spacecraft due to lack of solar orientation and subsequent battery drain. Contact between the spacecraft and mission control could not be established for over 24 hours.

Architecture, CPU, Memory, I/O

Three sets of computers, AIU, FC, and tbd. Two each.

Two redundant 1553 standard data buses, two solid state recorders with 1.1 gigabits and 0.67 gigabits respectively.

Software

80,000 lines of guidance and control code.

AIU: 21,000 lines of c code; 10,000 lines of assembly.

FC: 42,000 lines of ADA, 7,000 lines of assembly.

During the Anomaly Board review, seventeen software errors were uncovered. One of these which reported the momentum wheel speed as zero when it was actually at maximum. There were two different archived versions of the software flight load.

Sensors, Actuators

Five digital solar attitude detectors, an inertial measurement unit, (IMU) and a star tracker camera. Four reaction wheels for attitude control. Thrusters to dump angular momentum from the reaction wheels, and for rapid slew and propulsive maneuvers. Gyros.

Root Cause

Startup transient of the main engine exceeded an (incorrect) lateral acceleration safety threshold; leading to engine shutdown. There was a missing command in the burn-abort contingency script.

References

http://near.jhuapl.edu/

http://klabs.org/richcontent/Reports/Failure_Reports/NEAR_Rendezvous_Burn.pdf

"The NEAR Rendezvous Burn Anomaly of December 1990, Final Report of the NEAR (Near Earth Asteroid Rendezvous) Anomaly Review Board, Nov. 1999, JHU/APL.

Pioneer-10

The Pioneer-10 spacecraft was sent to study the far reaches of the solar system It passed through the Asteroid belt on its way to Jupiter and Saturn. It used a custom design, TTL discrete logic computer in 1972.

Exploring Comets

The Deep Impact mission returned images of the surface of comet Borrelly in 2001. That surface was hot (26-70C) , dry, and dark. In July of 2005, the same mission sent a probe into Comet Tempel 1. It created a crater, allowing imaging of subsurface material. Water ice was seen. Comet Borrely has a coma, which proved to be vaporized subsurface water ice. Deep Impact went on to complete a flyby of Comet Hartley-2 in 2010. The impactor used a RAD-750 flight computer with an imaging sensor, an inertial measurement unit, and four thrusters. It also included a star tracker, and an S-band communications link.

The 1999 Stardust mission retrieved sample material from the tail of Comet Wild 2 and returned it to Earth in 2006. The spacecraft computer was a RAD6000 with 128 megabytes of memory. The flight software took up 20% of the memory space, allowing for storing data when not in contact with Earth. The real time operating system was VxWorks. The comet material was captured in aerogel. Subsequently, 7 particles of interstellar dust were found in the aerogel. The mission also imaged the asteroids Annefrank, and was redirected to Tempel1 after the primary mission was complete. The RAD6000 cpu was used in the Command & Data Handling subsystem of Stardust.

ESA's Rosetta probe is in orbit around the comet Churyumov-Gerasimenko. It released a lander, Philae, which successfully touched down on the comet's surface in 2014. The onboard system has 3 gigabytes of solid state memory. The lander used a Harris RTX2020 processor. The lander communicated with the main spacecraft over a 32kbps link. It included dual 2 megabyte memories.

The memory size for the main processor was 1MWord RAM and 512 KWords EEPROM for each of 4 processors, and 512KWords PROM (redundant) accessible from each processor.

Clementine Spacecraft

The Clementine spacecraft suffered a catastrophic loss of propellant on May 7, 1994, leading to loss of the primary mission.

Architecture, CPU, Memory, I/O

Dual Command and Telemetry Processors (CTP), MIL-STD-1750A architecture

Sensors, Actuators

Dual star trackers, dual inertial measurement units, attitude control thrusters, reaction wheels.

Root Cause

The thrusters were erroneously held open for 11 minutes by the flight computer because the thruster protection timer (in software) contained an undetected bug. This depleted the spacecraft propellant.

References

nssdc.gsfc.nasa.gov/planetary/clementine.html

www.ganssle.com/watchdogs.pdf

Soyuz TMA-1 flight computer problem

The new guidance computer of the Russian Soyuz TMA-1 caused an off-course landing in its first use in 2003. This was a concern for the crew of the International Space Station, as the Soyuz TMA-2 was docked to the station as the crew return vehicle, and it had the same computer. The Soyuz is normally controlled to skim the atmosphere to reduce its velocity, using a deceleration of 5g's. The center of gravity of the craft is off center by design, and by rolling the capsule, the tilt, and thus the lift, can be controlled. As in the Apollo days, too steep, you burn up, and too shallow, you skip off the atmosphere and head back to space.

The TMS-1 autopilot lost its references, and switched to backup. This simple mode uses a roll maneuver to even out the path, while resulting in a deceleration twice that of the nominal mode, and a very short landing site, compared to the nominal. In this case, the crew returned safely, and were spotted by a rescue team within two hours.

It could have been worse. In 1965, the crew of the Voskhod-2, which had accomplished the first spacewalk, the capsule landed some 386 kilometers off course, and the crew had to spend the night in their capsule, due to the danger of bears and wolves in the area. Welcome back to Earth, tasty morsels!
Initially, the Soyuz error was attributed to the American crewman pushing the backup mode activation button, but this was later refuted by the crew, A software cause was sought. Software problems of potentially fatal effect had happened in 1988 (with the crew catching the error in time), and again in 1997, where two potentially catastrophic flaws were caught and mitigated by human intervention. One of these would have fired the reentry rockets in the wrong direction. The software has since been corrected. The Soyuz remains the main delivery and return vehicle for the mixed crew of the International Space Station.

Reference

Oberg, James "Software bug sent Soyuz off course," NBC News, MSNBC.com,

Phobos-Grunt

In November of 2010, the Russian Space Agency launched an ambitious mission to set a probe down on the small Martian moon Phobos, collect samples, and return them to Earth.

There was a failure of the spacecraft propulsion system that stranded the mission in Earth orbit. It re-entered the Earth's atmosphere in January 2011.

Various causes were postulated for the failure, including interference by U.S. Radar, cosmic ray induced upsets, programming errors, and counterfeit chips.

The final report from Roscosmos cited software errors, failure of chips in the electronics, possibly due to radiation damage, and the use of non-flight qualified electronics, with inadequate ground testing.

Evidently, identical chips in two assemblies failed nearly simultaneously, so quickly that an error message was not generated. It was possible that the error was recoverable, as the spacecraft entered a safe mode with a proper sun orientation for maximum power. However, the design precluded the reset mode before the spacecraft left its parking orbit. This was major design oversight.

The identified chips that failed were 512k SRAM chips. The part numbers from the Russian report were checked by NASA's Jet Propulsion Lab, and were found to be among the most radiation susceptible chips they had ever seen. Bad choice. The chips could last in space a few days, and were barely acceptable for non-critical applications, The probably failure cause was single event latch-up, which is sometimes recoverable.

References
Klotz, Irene "Programming Error Doomed Russian Mars Probe," Discovery News, Feb. 7, 2012, news.discovery.com

de Carbonnel, Alissa "Russia races to salvage stranded Mars probe, " Reuters, 2011. www.reuters.com
Amos, Jonathan "Phobos-Grunt mars Probe loses its way just after launch," 9 Nov. 2011, BBC News, www.bbc.co.uk

Oberg, James "Did Bad memory chips Down Russia's Mars Probe?," Feb 2012, IEEE Spectrum, IEEE.org.

Outer planet missions

The Gas giants are the planets Jupiter, Saturn, Uranus, and Neptune. These are the responsibility of the Jet Propulsion Laboratory, under contract to NASA. The RCA CMOS 1802 8-bit unit was used on JPL's Voyager, Viking and Galileo space probes. Prior to the Voyager mission, JPL was using simple sequencers purpose-built, and not based on a microprocessor architecture. This Command Computer System (CCS) architecture was 18-bit.

The Voyager missions were originally termed the "Grand tour" and were to have visited Mars, Jupiter, and Saturn, with possibly some of the outer planets as well. The mission was called MJS-77. Budget constraints caused the mission to refocus on Jupiter and Saturn alone. (In the interests of full disclosure, the author worked on the flight computer architecture for the MJS-77 mission.)

Voyager had a computer command subsystem (CCS) that controlled the imaging cameras. The CCS was based on an earlier design used for the Viking mission. The Attitude and Articulation control system (AACS) controlled the orientation of the spacecraft, and the movement of the camera platform. It is essentially the same computer as the CCS. The Data computer was constructed from a custom 4-bit CMOS component.

The ESA/NASA Ulysses mission visited the Jupiter system in 1992 and 2000, and collected data on the magnetosphere. This was a swing-by mission, as Ulysses was primarily to observe the Solar poles. Ulysses used a 280w RTG for power as it swung far from the Sun. Ulysses did not have a flight computer, but used Central Terminal Unit (CTU) and tape recorders for data storage. Each had a capacity of 45 megabits. The unit had an Attitude and Orbital Control System (AOCS), a purpose built unit, dual redundant, weighting 100 kilograms.

Cassini observed the planet from close-up in the year 2000, and studied the atmosphere. It used RTG's for power, and MIL-STD-1750A control computers.

Galileo entered Jupiter orbit in 1995, and returned data on the planet and the four Galilean moons until 2003. Three of the moons have thin atmospheres, and may have liquid water. The moon Ganymede has a magnetic field. Galileo was in the right place at the right time to see the comet Showmaker-

Levy-9 enter the Jovian atmosphere, and launched an atmospheric probe. Galileo used six of the 8-bit RCA 1802 microprocessors, operating at 1.6 MHz. These units had been fabricated on a sapphire substrate for radiation hardness. The Attitude and Articulation Control System used two bit-slice machines built from the AMD2901 chips.

Pluto

At this writing the New Horizons Mission (JHU-APL for NASA GSFC) has completed its flyby of Pluto, and is continuing to explore the fringes of the Solar System. Communications bandwidth is severely limited, and it will continue to send back the images it took for another year. The New Horizons Mission spacecraft carries two computer systems, the Command and Data Handling system and the Guidance and Control processor. Each of the two systems is duplicated for redundancy, for a total of four computers. The processor used is the Mongoose-V, a 12 MHz radiation-hardened version of the MIPS R3000 CPU. Multiple clocks and timing routines are implemented in hardware and software to help prevent faults and downtime. There are dual redundant machines for the C&DH function, and two more for Attitude control.

To conserve heat and mass, spacecraft and instrument electronics are housed together in IEMs (Integrated Electronics Modules). There are two redundant IEMs. Including other functions such as instrument and radio electronics, each IEM contains computers.

In March of 2007, the Command and Data Handling computer experienced an uncorrectable memory error and rebooted itself, causing the spacecraft to go into safe mode. The craft fully recovered within two days, with some data loss on Jupiter's magnetotail.

Wrap-up

Space missions are becoming increasingly complex as technology advances. The state of the art for space rated technology lags that of Earth based units by years because of the unique environments. Software doesn't fall into this category. Space missions can build on a huge and rapidly expanding base of technology. Our understanding of system complexity and failure modes is increasing every day, as embedded systems are being built into everything we touch on a daily basis.

From my phone, at this writing, I can talk to a cubesat, my watch, my washer and dryer, and my camera. Probably other stuff I am not aware of can talk to my phone.

The space environment is challenging, but we know how to cope with it. Everything ratchets up a few notches when manned flight is involved. It is attributed to Werner von Braun, that "Man is the best computer we can put aboard a spacecraft... and the only one that can be mass-produced with unskilled labor."

Man is also the most vulnerable. Human based exploration of space, with advanced technology tools is the future.

Glossary

1553 – Military standard data bus, serial, 1 Mbps.

6u – 6 units in size, where 1u is defined by dimensions and weight.

802.11 – a radio frequency wireless data communications standard.

AACS – (JPL) Attitude and articulation control system.

ACE – attitude control electronics

Actuator – device which converts a control signal to a mechanical action.

Ada – a computer language.

A/D, ADC – analog to digital converter

AFB – Air Force Base.

AGC – Automated guidance and control.

AIAA – American Institute of Aeronautics and Astronautics.

AIST – NASA GSFC Advanced Information System Technology .

ALU – arithmetic logic unit.

AmSat – Amateur Satellite. Favored by Ham Radio operators as communication relays.

Analog – concerned with continuous values.

ANSI – American National Standards Institute

Android – an operating system based on Gnu-Linux, popular for smart phones and tablet computers.

AOP – Advanced onboard processor (NASA/GSFC).

AP – application programs.

AP-101 – Based on IBM S/360 technology, the computers on the Space shuttle.

API – application program interface; specification for software modules to communicate.

APL – Applied Physics Laboratory, of the Johns Hopkins University.

Apollo – US manned lunar program.

Arduino – a small, inexpensive microcontroller architecture.

Arinc – Aeronautical Radio, Inc. commercial company supporting transportation, and providing standards for avionics.

ARM – Acorn RISC machine; a 32-bit architecture with wide application in embedded systems.

ARPA – (U. S.) Advanced Research Projects Agency.

ArpaNet – Advanced Research Projects Agency (U.S.), first packet switched network, 1968.

ASIC – application specific integrated circuit

async – non synchronized

ATAC – Applied Technologies Advanced Computer.

AU – astronomical unit. Roughly 93 million miles, the mean distance between Earth and Sun,

BAE – British Aerospace.

Baud – symbol rate; may or may not be the same as bit rate.

BCD – binary coded decimal. 4-bit entity used to represent 10 different decimal digits; with 6 spare states.

Beowolf – a cluster of commodity computer chips'; multiprocessor.

Big-endian – data format with the most significant bit or byte at the lowest address, or transmitted first.

Binary – using base 2 arithmetic for number representation.

BIST – built-in self test.

Bit – binary variable, value of 1 or 0.

Boolean – a data type with two values; an operation on these data types; named after George Boole, mid-19th century inventor of Boolean algebra.

Bootloader – initial program run after power-on or reset. Gets the computer up & going.

Bootstrap – a startup or reset process that proceeds without external intervention.

BSD – Berkeley Software Distribution version of the Bell Labs Unix operating system.

BP - bundle protocol, for dealing with errors and disconnects.

BSP – board support package. Customization Software and device drivers.

Buffer – a temporary holding location for data.

Bug – an error in a program or device.

Bus – an electrical connection between 2 or more units; the engineering part of the spacecraft.

byte – a collection of 8 bits

C – programming language from Bell Labs, circa 1972.

cache – temporary storage between cpu and main memory.

Cache coherency – process to keep the contents of multiple caches consistent,

CAN - controller area network bus.

CCSDS – Consultive Committee on Space Data Systems.

C&DH – Command and Data Handling

CDFP CCSDS File Delivery Protocol

cFE – Core Flight Executive.

CFS – Core Flight Software.

Chip – integrated circuit component.

Clock – periodic timing signal to control and synchronize operations.

CME – Coronal Mass Ejection. Solar storm.

CMOS – complementary metal oxide semiconductor; a technology using both positive and negative semiconductors to achieve low power operation.

Complement – in binary logic, the opposite state.

Compilation – software process to translate source code to assembly or machine code (or error codes).

Configware – equivalent of software for FPGA architectures; configuration information.

Control Flow – computer architecture involving directed flow through the program; data dependent paths are allowed.

COP – computer operating properly.

Coprocessor – another processor to supplement the operations of the main processor. Used for floating point, video, etc. Usually relies on the main processor for instruction fetch; and control.

Cordic – Coordinate Rotation Digital Computer – to calculate hyberbolic and trig functions.

Cots – commercial, off the shelf

CPU – central processing unit

CRC – cyclic redundancy code – error detection and correction mechanism.

Cubesat – small inexpensive satellite for colleges, high schools, and individuals.

D/A – digital to analog conversion.

DAC – digital to analog converter.

Daemon – in multitasking, a program that runs in the background.

DARPA – Defense advanced research projects agency.

Dataflow – computer architecture where a changing value forces recalculation of dependent values.

Datagram – message on a packet switched network; the delivery, arrival time, and order of arrival are not guaranteed.

dc – direct current.

D-cache – data cache.

DDR – dual data rate memory.

Deadlock – a situation in which two or more competing actions are each waiting for the other to finish, and thus neither ever does.

DCE – data communications equipment; interface to the network.

Deadly embrace – a deadlock situation in which 2 processes are each waiting for the other to finish.

Denorm – in floating point representation, a non-zero number with a magnitude less than the smallest normal number.

Device driver – specific software to interface a peripheral to the operating system.

Digital – using discrete values for representation of states or numbers.

Dirty bit – used to signal that the contents of a cache have changed.

Discrete – single bit signal.

DMA – direct memory access.

DOD – (U. S.) Department of Defense.

DOE – (U. S.) Department of Energy

Downlink – from space to earth.

Dram – dynamic random access memory.

DSP – digital signal processing/processor.

DTE – data terminal equipment; communicates with the DCE to get to the network.

DTN – delay tolerant networks.

DUT – device under test.

ECC – error correcting code

EDAC – error detecting and correction circuitry.

EDAC – error detection and correction.

EIA – Electronics Industry Association.

Embedded system – a computer systems with limited human interfaces and performing specific tasks. Usually part of a larger system.

EOS – Earth Observation spacecraft.

Ephemeris – orbital position data.

Epitaxial – in semiconductors, have a crystalline overlayer with a well-defined orientation.

Eps – electrical power subsystem.

ESA – European Space Organization.

ESRO – European Space Research Organization

ESTO – NASA/GSFC – Earth Science Technology Office.

Ethernet – networking protocol, IEEE 802.3

ev – electron volt, unit of energy

EVA – extra-vehicular activity.

Exception – interrupt due to internal events, such as overflow.

FAA – (U. S.) Federal Aviation Administration.

Fail-safe – a system designed to do no harm in the event of failure.

Falcon – launch vehicle from SpaceX.

FDC – fault detection and correction.

Firewire – IEEE-1394 standard for serial communication.

Firmware – code contained in a non-volatile memory.

Fixed point – computer numeric format with a fixed number of digits or bits, and a fixed radix point. Integers.

Flag – a binary state variable.

Flash – non-volatile memory

Flatsat – prototyping and test setup, laid out on a bench for easy access.

FlightLinux – NASA Research Program for Open Source code in space.

Floating point – computer numeric format for real numbers; has significant digits and an exponent.

FPGA – field programmable gate array.

FPU – floating point unit, an ALU for floating point numbers.

Full duplex – communication in both directions simultaneously.

Fram – ferromagnetic RAM; a non-volatile memory technology

FSW – flight software.

FTP – file transfer protocol

Gbyte – 10^9 bytes.

GEO – geosynchronous orbit.

GeV – billion (10^9) electron volts

Gnu – recursive acronym, gnu is not unix.

GPL – gnu public license used for free software; referred to as the "copyleft."

GPS – Global Positioning system – Navigation satellites.

GPU – graphics processing unit. ALU for graphics data.

GSFC – Goddard Space Flight Center, Greenbelt, MD.

Gyro – (gyroscope) a sensor to measure rotation.

Half-duplex – communications in two directions, but not simultaneously.

HAL/S – computer language.

Handshake – co-ordination mechanism.

HDL – hardware description language

Hertz – cycles per second.

Hexadecimal – base 16 number representation.

HPCC – High Performance Computing and Communications.

Hypervisor – virtual machine manager. Can manage multiple operating systems.

I-cache – Instruction cache.

IC&DH – Instrument Command & Data Handling.

IEEE – Institute of Electrical and Electronic engineers

IEEE-754 – standard for floating point representation and calculation.

IIC – inter-integrated circuit (I/O).

Integer – the natural numbers, zero, and the negatives of the natural numbers.

Interrupt – an asynchronous event to signal a need for attention (example: the phone rings).

Interrupt vector – entry in a table pointing to an interrupt service routine; indexed by interrupt number.

IP – intellectual property; Internet protocol.

IP core – IP describing a chip design that can be licensed to be used in an FPGA or ASIC.

IP-in-Space – Internet Protocol in Space.

IR – infrared, 1-400 terahertz. Perceived as heat.

ISA – instruction set architecture, the software description of the computer.

ISO – International Standards Organization.

ISR – interrupt service routine, a subroutine that handles a particular interrupt event.

ISS – International Space Station

ITAR – International Trafficking in Arms Regulations (US Dept. of State)

IV&V – Independent validation and verification.

JHU – Johns Hopkins University.

JPL – Jet Propulsion Laboratory

JSC – Johnson Space Center, Houston, Texas.

JTAG – Joint Test Action Group; industry group that lead to IEEE 1149.1, Standard Test Access Port and Boundary-Scan Architecture.

JWST – James Webb Space Telescope – follow on to Hubble.

Kbps – kilo (10^3) bits per second.

Kernel – main portion of the operating system. Interface between the applications and the hardware.

Kg – kilogram.

kHz – kilo (10^3) hertz

KVA – kilo volts amps – a measure of electrical power

Ku band – 12-18 Ghz radio

Lan – local area network, wired or wireless

LaRC – (NASA) Langley Research Center.

Latchup – condition in which a semiconductor device is stuck in one state.

Lbf – pounds-force.

LEO – low Earth orbit.

Let- Linear Energy Transfer

Lidar – optical radar.

Linux – open source operating system.

List – a data structure.

Little-endian – data format with the least significant bit or byte at the highest address, or transmitted last.

Logic operation – generally, negate, AND, OR, XOR, and their inverses.

Loop-unrolling – optimization of a loop for speed at the cost of space.

LRU – least recently used; an algorithm for item replacement in a cache.

LSB – least significant bit or byte.

LUT – look up table.

Master-slave – control process with one element in charge. Master status may be exchanged among elements.

Mbps – mega (10^6) bits per second.

Mbyte – one million (10^6 or $2^{20)}$ bytes.

Memory leak – when a program uses memory resources but does not return them, leading to a lack of available memory.

Memory scrubbing – detecting and correcting bit errors.

MEMS – Micro Electronic Mechanical System.

MESI – modified, exclusive, shared, invalid state of a cache coherency protocol.

MEV – million electron volts.

MHz – one million (10^6) Hertz

Microcontroller – monolithic cpu + memory + I/O.

Microkernel – operating system which is not monolithic, functions execute in user space.

Microprocessor – monolithic cpu.

Microsat – satellite with a mass between 10 and 100 kg.

Microsecond – 10^{-6} second.

Microkernel – operating system which is not monolithic. So functions execute in user space.

mram – magnetorestrictive random access memory.

mSec – Millisecond; (10^{-3}) second.

MIPS – millions of instructions per second.

MMU – memory management unit; manned maneuvering unit.

MSB – most significant bit or byte.

Multiplex – combining signals on a communication channel by sampling.

Multicore – multiple processing cores on one substrate or chip; need not be identical.

Mutex – a software mechanism to provide mutual exclusion between tasks.

Nano – 10^{-9}

nanoSat – small satellite with a mass between 1 and 10 kg.

NASA - National Aeronautics and Space Administration.

NDA – non-disclosure agreement; legal agreement protecting IP.

Nibble – 4 bits, ½ byte.

NIST – National Institute of Standards and Technology (US), previously, National Bureau of Standards.

NMI – non-maskable interrupt; cannot be ignored by the software.

Normalized number – in the proper format for floating point representation.

NRE – non-recurring engineering; one-time costs for a project.

NSF – (U.S.) National Science Foundation.

NUMA – non-uniform memory access for multiprocessors; local and global memory access protocol.

NVM – non-volatile memory.

Nyquist rate – in communications, the minimum sampling rate, equal to twice the highest frequency in the signal.

OBC – on board computer

OBD – On-Board diagnostics.

OBP – On Board Processor

Off-the-shelf – commercially available; not custom.

OpAmp – (Linear) operational amplifier; linear gain and isolation stage.

OpCode – encoded computer instruction.

Open source – methodology for hardware or software development with free distribution and access.

Operating system – software that controls the allocation of resources in a computer.

OSAL – operating system abstraction layer.

OSI – Open systems interconnect model for networking, from ISO.

Overflow - the result of an arithmetic operation exceeds the capacity of the destination.

Packet – a small container; a block of data on a network.

Paging – memory management technique using fixed size memory blocks.

Paradigm – a pattern or model

Paradigm shift – a change from one paradigm to another. Disruptive or evolutionary.

Parallel – multiple operations or communication proceeding simultaneously.

Parity – an error detecting mechanism involving an extra check bit in the word.

Pc – personal computer.

PCB – printed circuit board.

pci – personal computer interface (bus).

PCM – pulse code modulation.

Peta - 10^{15} or 2^{50}

Phonesat – small satellite using a cell phone for onboard control and computation.

Picosat – small satellite with a mass between 0.1 and 1 kg.

Piezo – production of electricity by mechanical stress.

Pinout – mapping of signals to I/O pins of a device.

Pipeline – operations in serial, assembly-line fashion.

Pixel – picture element; smallest addressable element on a display or a sensor.

PLL – phase locked loop.

POSIX – IEEE standard operating system.

PPL – preferred parts list (NASA).

Psia – pounds per square inch, absolute.

PSP – Platform Support Package.

PWM – pulse width modulation.

Python – programming language.

Quadrature encoder – an incremental rotary encoder providing rotational position information.

Queue – first in, first out data buffer structure; implemented in hardware or software.

Rad – unit of radiation exposure

Rad750 – A radiation hardened IBM PowerPC cpu.

Radix point – separates integer and fractional parts of a real number.

RAID – redundant array of inexpensive disks.

Ram – random access memory.

Real-time – system that responds to events in a predictable, bounded time.

Register – temporary storage location for a data item.

Reset – signal and process that returns the hardware to a known, defined state.

RF – radio frequency

RFC – request for comment

RISC – reduced instruction set computer.

RHPPC – Rad-Hard Power PC.

RISC – reduced instruction set computer.

Router – networking component for packets.

RS-232/422/423 – asynchronous and synchronous serial communication standards.

RT – remote terminal.

RTOS – real time operating system.

SAM – sequential access memory, like a magnetic tape.

Sandbox – an isolated and controlled environment to run untested or potentially malicious code.

SCADA – Supervisory Control and Data Acquisition – for industrial control systems.

SDR – software defined radio

SDRAM – synchronous dynamic random access memory.

Segmentation – dividing a network or memory into sections.

Semiconductor – material with electrical characteristics between conductors and insulators; basis of current technology processor, memory, and I/O devices, as well as sensors.

Semaphore – a binary signaling element among processes.

SDVF – Software Development and Validation Facility.

Sensor – a device that converts a physical observable quantity or event to a signal.

Serial – bit by bit.

SEU – single event upset (radiation induced error).

Servo – a control device with feedback.

SIMD – single instruction, multiple data (parallel processing)

SOC – system on a chip; also state-of-charge.

Socket – an end-point in communication across a network

Soft core – a hardware description language description of a cpu core.

Socket – an end-point in communication across a network

Software – set of instructions and data to tell a computer what to do.

SMP – symmetric multiprocessing.

Snoop – monitor packets in a network, or data in a cache.

SRAM – static random access memory.

Stack – first in, last out data structure. Can be hardware or software.

Stack pointer – a reference pointer to the top of the stack.

STAR – self test and repair.

State machine – model of sequential processes.

STOL – system test oriented language, a scripting language for testing systems.

T&I – test and integration.

Terrabyte – 10^{12} bytes.

SAA – South Atlantic anomaly. High radiation zone.

SEU – single event upset.

Soc – state of charge; system on a chip.

Soft core – hardware description description language model of a logic core.

SoS – silicon on sapphire – an inherently radiation-hard technology

spi – serial peripheral interface

SSTL – Surrey Space Technology Labs (UK).

SpaceCube – an advanced FPGA-based flight computer.

SpaceWire – networking and interconnect standard.

Space-X – commercial space company.

SRAM – static random access memory.

Stack – first in, last out data structure. Can be hardware or software.

Stack pointer – a reference pointer to the top of the stack.

State machine – model of sequential processes.

Superscalar – computer with instruction-level parallelism, by replication of resources.

SWD – serial wire debug.

Synchronous – using the same clock to coordinate operations.

System – a collection of interacting elements and relationships with a specific behavior.

System of Systems – a complex collection of systems with pooled resources.

Suitsat – old Russian spacesuit, instrumented and launched from the ISS.

sync – synchronize, synchronized.

TCP/IP – Transmission Control Protocol/Internet protocol.

TDRSS – Tracking and Data Relay satellite system.

Tera - 10^{12} or 2^{40}

Test-and-set – coordination mechanism for multiple processes that allows reading to a location and writing it in a non-interruptible manner.

TCP/IP – transmission control protocol/internet protocol; layered set of protocols for networks.

Thread – smallest independent set of instructions managed by a multiprocessing operating system.

TMR – triple modular redundancy.

Toolchain – set of software tools for development.

Transceiver – receiver and transmitter in one box.

Transducer – a device that converts one form of energy to another.

TRAP – exception or fault handling mechanism in a computer; an operating system component.

Triplicate – using three copies (of hardware, software, messaging, power supplies, etc.). for redundancy and error control.

Truncate – discard. cutoff, make shorter.

ttl – transistor-transistor logic integrated circuit.

UART – Universal asynchronous receiver-transmitter.

UDP – User datagram protocol; part of the Internet Protocol.

uM – micro (10^{-6}) meter

Underflow – the result of an arithmetic operation is smaller than the smallest representable number.

UoSat – a family of small spacecraft from Surrey Space Technology Ltd. (UK).

uplink – from ground to space.

USAF – United States Air Force.

Usb – universal serial bus.

VDC – volts, direct current.

Vector – single dimensional array of values.

VHDL – very high level design language.

VIA – vertical conducting pathway through an insulating layer.

Virtual memory – memory management technique using address translation.

Virtualization – creating a virtual resource from available physical resources.

Virus – malignant computer program.

Viterbi Decoder – a maximum likelihood decoder for data encoded with a Convolutional code for error control. Can be implemented in software or hardware

VLIW – very long instruction word – mechanism for parallelism.

VxWorks – real time operating systems from Wind River systems.

WiFi – short range digital radio.

Watchdog – hardware/software function to sanity check the hardware, software, and process; applies corrective action if a fault is detected; fail-safe mechanism.

Wiki – the Hawaiian word for "quick." Refers to a collaborative content website.

Wind River – commercial real time operating system vendor.

Word – a collection of bits of any size; does not have to be a power of two.

Write-back – cache organization where the data is not written to main memory until the cache location is needed for re-use.

Write-through – all cache writes also go to main memory.

X-band – 7 – 11 GHz.

Xilinx – manufacturer of programmable logic and FPGA's.

Zener – voltage reference diode.

Zero address – architecture using implicit addressing, like a stack.

References

Barr, Michael; Massa, Anthony; *Programming Embedded Systems: With C and GNU Development Tools*, 2nd Edition O'Reilly Media, Inc.; 2nd edition, 2006, ISBN-0596009836.

Barnhart, David J Major, "Satellite on-a-Chip Feasibility for Distributed Space Missions," U. Surrey, July 2006, Report C104-1825, U.S. Dept of the Air Force.

Boswell, David. "The Software of Space Exploration," 3/30/2006. www.onlamo.com/pub/a/onlamp/2006/0-3/30/Software of space exploration.html

Chisnall, David "Optimizing Code for Power Consumption," Nov. 18, 2010, Addison-Wesley Prof, www.informit.com/articles/

Cressler, John D. (Ed), H. Mantooth, Alan (Ed) *Extreme Environment Electronics*, 1st Edition, CRC Press; 1 edition, 2012, ISBN-1439874301.

Cudmore, Alan NASA/GSFC's Flight Software Architecture: core Flight Executive and Core Flight System, NASA/GSFC Code 582.

DeCoursey, R.; Melton, Ryan; Estes, Robert R. Jr. "Sensors, Systems, and Next-Generation Satellites X," Proceedings of the SPIE, Vol. 6361 pp 63611m (2006). (use of non-radiation hardened cpus).

Del Castillo, Linda et al *Extreme Environment Electronic Packaging for Venus and Mars Landed Missions,* JPL, https://solarsystem.nasa.gov/docs/7_8DELCASTILLO_paper.pdf

Eickhoff, Jens *Onboard Computers, Onboard Software and Satellite Operations: An Introduction*, 2011, Springer Aerospace Technology, ISBN-3642251692.

Fesq, Lorraine; Dvorak, Dan NASA's Software Architecture Review Board's (SARB) Findings from the Review of GSFC's "core Flight Executive/Core Flight Software" (cFE/CFS), NASA Software Architecture Review Board , Flight Software Workshop, Nov 7-9, 2012.

Finckenor, Miria M., de Groh, Kim *Space Environmental Effects, A Researcher's Guide to International Space Station,* NASA ISS Program Office.

Fortescue, Peter and Stark, John *Spacecraft System Engineering,* 2nd ed, Wiley, 1995, ISBN 0-471-95220-6.

Foudriat, E. C., Senn, E. H., Will, R. W., Straeter, T. A., "A Progress Report on a NASA Research Program for Embedded Computer Systems Software," AIAA Paper 79-1956, 1979.

Fowler, Kim *Mission-Critical and Safety-Critical Systems Handbook: Design and Development for Embedded Applications,* Newnes; 1st edition, November 20, 2009, ISBN- 0750685670.

Ganssle, Jack *The Art of Programming Embedded Systems* Publisher: Academic Press; 1st edition, 1991, ISBN 0122748808.

Ganssle, Jack *Embedded Systems, World Class Designs,* Newnes; 1st edition, 2007, ISBN- 0750686251.

Gasperson, Tina, "FlightLinux blasts off again," Linux.com, July 03, 2007.

Gaudin, Sharon "NASA upgrades Mars Curiosity software… from 350M miles away," Computerworld, article 9230151.

Geer, Dwight A. "System Flight Computer," June 6, 2001, NASA/JPL, Europa Orbiter/X2000 Avionics Industry Briefing.

Ghahroodi. Massoud M., Ozer, Emre, Bull, David *SEU and SET-tolerant ARM Cortex-R$ CPU for Space and Avionics Applications, www.median-project.eu/wp-content/.../median2013_submission_5.pdf*

Goforth, Montgomery *NASA Avionics Architectures for Exploration (AAE) and Fault Tolerant Computing,* Document ID: 20140008709, 2014, JSC-CN-31331.

Gruen, Jim, "Linux in Space," 8/24/12, SpaceX.

Harland, David M. and Lorenz, Ralph D. *Space Systems Failures, Disasters and Rescues of Satellites, Rockets and Space Probes,*. 2005, Praxis Publishing, ISBN 0-387-21519-0.

Hennessy, John L. and Patterson, David A. *Computer Architecture, Fifth Edition: A Quantitative Approach*, Morgan Kaufmann,, 2011, ISBN 012383872X.

Holmes-Siedle, A. G. and Adams, L. *Handbook of Radiation Effects*, 2002, Oxford University Press, ISBN 0-19-850733-X.

Jones, Dr. Robert L. and Hodson, Dr. Robert F. "A Roadmap for the Development of Reconfigurable Computing for Space," March 23, 2007, NASA-Langley Research Center.

Judas, Paul A.; Prokop, Lorraine E. "A Historical Compilation of Software Metrics with Applicability to NASA's Orion Spacecraft Flight Software Sizing,"in Innovations in Systems and Software Engineering, 2011, 7:161-170, Springer.

Kalinsky, David, "Architecture of Safety-Critical Systems," Aug 23. 2005, available white paper at www.embedded.com.

Kurzak, Jakub; Bader, David A.; Dongarra, Jack (Eds) *Scientific Computing with Multicore and Accelerators* CRC Press; 1 edition, 2010, ISBN 143982536X.

Labrosse, Jean J.; Ganssle, Jack; Oshana, Robert; Walls, Colin; *Embedded Software*, Newnes, 200,7 ISBN-978-0750685832.

Lamie, Edward *Real-Time Embedded Multithreading Using ThreadX and ARM*, Newnes; 2nd edition, 2009, ISBN 1856176010.

Leveson, Nancy G. "Software Safety in Embedded Computer Systems," Communications of the ACM. Vol. 34, No. 2, February 1991, pp. 34-46.

Marquart, Jane "Flight Software Technology Roadmap, NASA/GSFC, 1998.

Messenger, G. C. and Ash, M. S. *The Effects of Radiation on Electronic Systems,* 1992, Van Nostrand Reinhold.

137

Pan, Jiantao, *Software Reliability*, Carnegie Mellon University, course 18-849b, Dependable Embedded Systems.

Patterson, David A and Hennessy, John L. *Computer Organization and Design: The Hardware/Software Interface*, ARM Edition, Morgan Kaufmann, 2011, ISBN 8131222748.

Petersen, Edward *Single Event Effects in Aerospace* 1st Ed. Wiley-IEEE Press; 1 edition, October 4, 2011, ISBN- 0470767499.

Sahu, Kusum, *EEE-INST-002, Instructions for EEE Parts Selection, Screening, Qualification, and Derating*, with addendum 1, April 2008, NASA/TP-2003-212242.

Sheppard, Andrew *Programming GPUs* 2011, O'Reilly Media, ISBN 1449302351.

Simon, David E. *An Embedded Software Primer*, Addison-Wesley Professional, 1990, ISBN 020161569X.

Stakem, Patrick H. *The History of Spacecraft Computers from the V-2 to the Space Station*, 2013, PRRB Publishing, ASIN B004L626U6.

Stakem, Patrick H. *Apollo's Computers,* 2014, PRRB Publishing, ASIN B00LDT217.

Stakem, Patrick H. *Microprocessors in Space*, 2011, PRRB Publishing, ASIN: B0057PFJQI.

Stakem, Patrick H. "A Survey of On-Board Satellite Computers," Orbital Systems, LTD, whitepaper, 1982.

Stakem, Patrick H. "Operational Experience with Support of a Programmable Spacecraft Onboard Computer," Proc. IEEE Southeastcon, 1977.

Stakem, Patrick H. "Migration of an Image Classification Algorithm to an Onboard Computer for Downlink Data Reduction," AIAA Journal of Aerospace Computing, Information, and Communication , Feb 2004 ,Vol. 1 no. 2 pp 108-111.

Stakem, Patrick H. "Linux in Space", Oct. 2, 2003, invited presentation, Institution of Electrical Engineers, Sheffield Hallam University, Sheffield, UK.

Stakem, Patrick H. "The Applications of Computers and Microprocessors Onboard Spacecraft, NASA/GSFC 1980.

Stakem, Patrick H. "Free Software in Space–the NASA Case," invited paper, Software Livre 2002, May 3, 2002, Porto Allegre, Brazil.

Stallings, William *Computer Organization and Architecture: Designing for Performance* (7th Edition), Prentice Hall; 7 edition (July 21, 2005) ISBN 0131856448.

Stevenson, David "Next Generation Embedded Processors Empower Satellite Telemetry and Command Systems, Aeroflex, Colorado Springs, www.aeroflex.com/RadHard

Violette, Daniel P. "Arduino/Raspberry Pi: Hobbyist Hardware and Radiation Total Dose Degradation," 2014, presented at the EEE Parts for Small Missions Conference, NASA-GSFC, Greenbelt, MD, September 10-11, 2014.

Wertz, James R. (ed) *Spacecraft Attitude Determination and Control*, section 6.9, Onboard Computers, 1980, Kluwer, ISBN 90-277-1204-2.

Wichmann, Brian A. *Software in Safety Related Systems*, Wiley, 1992. ISBN 0471-93474-7.

Wolf, Marilyn *High-Performance Embedded Computing, Applications in cyber-Physical Systems and Mobile Computing*, 2nd ed, 2014, Morgan Kaufmann, ISBN 978-0-12-410511-9.

Wooster, Paul; Boswell, David; Stakem, Patrick; Cowan-Sharp, Jessy "Open Source Software for Small Satellites," SSC07-XII-3, 21st. Annual AIAA/USU, paper SSC07-XII-3, July 2007.

Resources

Small Spacecraft Technology State of the Art, NASA-Ames, NASA/tp-2014-

216648/REV1, July 2014.

NASA Office of Logic Design, Spaceborne Processor and Avionics Papers, http://www.solarstorms.org/SEUcomputers.html

wikipedia, various. Material from Wikipedia (www.wikipedia.org) is used under the conditions of the Creative commons Attribution-ShareAlike #.0 Unported License.
http://creativecommons.org/licenses/by-sa/3.0

http://grouper.ieee.org/groups/754/

The Flight Software Workshops (FSW-xx) has been held since 2007, generally alternating between the East Coast and the West Coast. The Aerospace Corporation, NASA Jet Propulsion Laboratory, The Johns Hopkins University Applied Physics Laboratory and Southwest Research Institute are the Founding Sponsors of the Flight Software Workshops. http://flightsoftware.jhuapl.edu/index.html

Core Flight System (CFS) Deployment Guide, Ver. 2.8, 9/30/2010, NASA/GSFC 582-2008-012.

NASA Scientific and Technical Information Program, http://www.sti.nasa.gov/

www.ARM.com

www.ccsds.org

If you enjoyed this book, you might find something else from the author interesting as well. Available on Amazon Kindle.

16-bit Microprocessors, History and Architecture, 2013 PRRB Publishing, ASIN B00D5ETQ3U.

4- and 8-bit Microprocessors, Architecture and History, 2013, PRRB Publishing, ASIN B00D5ZSKCC.

Apollo's Computers, 2014, PRRB Publishing, ASIN B00LDT217.

The Architecture and Applications of the ARM Microprocessors, 2013, PRRB Publishing, ASIN B00BAFF4OQ.

Earth Rovers: for Exploration and Environmental Monitoring, 2014, PRRB Publishing, ASIN BOOMBKZCBE.

Embedded Computer Systems, Volume 1, Introduction and Architecture, 2013, PRRB Publishing, ASIN B00GB0W4GG.

The History of Spacecraft Computers from the V-2 to the Space Station, 2013, PRRB Publishing, ASIN B004L626U6.

Floating Point Computation, 2013, PRRB Publishing, ASIN B00D5E1S7W.

Architecture of Massively Parallel Microprocessor Systems, 2011, PRRB Publishing, ASIN B004K1F172.

Multicore Computer Architecture, 2014, PRRB Publishing, ASIN B00KB2XIQD.

Personal Robots, 2014, PRRB Publishing, ASIN BOOMBQ084K.

RISC Microprocessors, History and Overview, 2013, PRRB Publishing, ASIN B00D5SCHQO.

Robots and Telerobots in Space Applications, 2011, PRRB Publishing, ASIN B0057IMJRM.

The Saturn Rocket and the Pegasus Missions, 1965, 2013, PRRB Publishing, ASIN B00BVA79ZW.

Microprocessors in Space, 2011, PRRB Publishing, ASIN B0057PFJQI.

Computer Virtualization and the Cloud, 2013, PRRB Publishing, ASIN B00BAFF0JA.

What's the Worst That Could Happen? Bad Assumptions, Ignorance, Failures and Screw-ups in Engineering Projects, 2014, PRRB Publishing, ASIN

B00J7SH540.

Computer Architecture & Programming of the Intel x86 Family, 2013, PRRB Publishing, ASIN B0078Q39D4.

The Hardware and Software Architecture of the Transputer, 2011, PRRB Publishing, ASIN B004OYTS1K.

Mainframes, Computing on Big Iron, 2015, PRRB Publishing, ASIN B00TXQQ3FI

Spacecraft Control Center, 2015, PRRB Publishing, due 2016..

A Practitioner's Guide to RISC Microprocessor Architecture, Wiley-Interscience, 1996, ISBN 0471130184.

www.ingramcontent.com/pod-product-compliance
Lightning Source LLC
LaVergne TN
LVHW042124070326
832902LV00036B/654